OTHER BOOKS BY ROGER FRITZ

What Managers Need to Know

Productivity and Results (12 Book Series)

Performance Based Management

Rate Yourself as a Manager

You're in Charge: A Guide for Business and Personal Success

The Inside Advantage

Nobody Gets Rich Working for Somebody Else

Personal Performance Contracts

*If They Can—You Can! Lessons from America's New Breed
of Successful Entrepreneurs*

Rate Your Executive Potential

Management Ideas That Work

How to Export: Everything You Need to Know to Get Started

Ready, Aim, HIRE! (Co-author)

*The Entrepreneurial Family: How to Sustain the Vision
and Value in Your Family Business*

Family Ties and Business Binds: How to Solve the Inevitable

Problems of Family Businesses

Think Like a Manager

Sleep Disorders: America's Hidden Nightmare

*Sales Manager's High Performance Guide: The Only Reference
You Need to Build a Powerful Sales Force*

A Team of Eagles

How to Manage Your Boss

The Small Business Troubleshooter

Wars of Successio

D0189137

Fast Track: How to Gain and Keep Momentum

One Step Ahead: The Unused Keys to Success

Bounce Back and Win: What It Takes and How to Do It

Magnet People: Their Secrets and How to Learn From Them

Little Things—Big Results:
How Small Events Determine Our Fate

How to Make Your Boss Your Ally and Advocate

Building Your Legacy: One Decision at a Time

100 Ways to Bring Out Your Best

After You: Can Humble People Prevail?

Sharpen Your Competitive Edge

Nothing Ventured, Nothing Gained

Who Cares: Are You a Giver, Taker, or Watcher?

Why Stop Now: Resisting the Temptation to Retreat

The Power of a Positive Attitude:
Discovering the Key to Success

Successful Sales Management: How to
Build and Lead a Successful Sales Team

Make Yourself Needed:
Self Management Equals Sales Success

The Challenge of Change

ON CD-ROM

The Personal Business Coach

Beyond Commitment: The Skills All Leaders Need

Stand and Deliver...

or Step Aside

*"The difference between yesterday and tomorrow is made by those who **Stand and Deliver** today."*

Stand and Deliver...
or Step Aside

Roger Fritz

Inside Advantage Publications
Naperville, Illinois

Published by:
Inside Advantage Publications
1240 Iroquois Drive, Suite 406
Naperville, IL 60563
Phone: 630-420-7673
Fax: 630-420-7835
rfritz3800@aol.com
http:://www.rogerfritz.com

Unless specifically noted by naming others, all quotations are attributable to the author, Roger Fritz.

http://www.rogerfritz.com

Inside Advantage Publications
Naperville, Illinois

ISBN-13: 987-1-893987-32-6

Contents

For my Grandfather, Ole Sandley,
whose indelible boyhood
example for me, while doing
daily farm chores was:
"I'll show you now, then you do it!"
In other words—"Stand and Deliver."

Acknowledgments

This book moved from incubation to reality with critical help at various times from:

Nancy Fritz, whose judgment is always dependable.

Marsha Portnoy, whose special organizational skills and ideas are so helpful.

Dan Runty, for persistence through many manuscript changes.

Publishers Graphics for their fine printing work and service.

Sans Serif, Inc. for creative text and cover design.

Introduction

Few things in life are always reliable but one fact seems clear. Any time you look back you see it— *all progress depends not on those who watch and wait, but on those who stand and deliver.*

Since childhood, I have been curious about why things tend to stay the same until one individual comes along who creates change. I have been even more fascinated by:

~ Why some changes last but many do not.
~ Why some initiators are adored and some despised.
~ Why some results are good and some bad.
~ Why some groups resist change more than others.
~ Why level of formal education or credentials doesn't seem to make any difference in receptivity to change.
~ Why change resisters have more credibility than risk takers.
~ How bold leaders retain confidence.
~ How the best leaders prepare people to stimulate change from within before it is forced upon them.

This book focuses on what I believe are the qualities of people who will **Stand and Deliver**.

At the same time it examines the reasons for and results of withdrawal. Hopefully, it will be helpful as a type of benchmark for many who are uncertain about themselves and willing to move forward now.

—Roger Fritz

1

Winners and Leaders Prepare

The only time leadership is accidental is in an emergency. It may last during the crisis, but usually not after. The reason? The daring and quick response required in an emergency will not be enough to sustain leadership when circumstances are normal. That requires preparation and the cultivation of many other critical skills and attributes. These have met the test of time:

The Qualities of Effective Leaders (Do You Have Them?)

Accountability—They seek responsibility and accept risks.

Presentation—Face-to-face, they are able to express themselves clearly and persuasively.

Written communication—They convey essential information accurately.

Innovation—They are a source of new ideas and creative solutions.

Versatility—Their interests, talents and experiences are varied.

Conflict tolerance—They are a stable influence in times of stress.

Organization—They are orderly in thought and action.

Listening—They distill needed information.

Empathy—They are sensitive to others' needs.

Initiative—They try new ways without needing orders or direction.

Adaptability—They modify their actions to achieve goals.

Persistence—They persevere through difficulty.

Objectivity—They set measurable goals and prefer facts vs. opinions.

Performance standards—They continuously raise accomplishment levels.

Respect—They've earned it through their integrity, honesty and moral soundness.

Underlying these principles are five fundamental qualities needed to prepare for leadership.

1. Leaders Look for Unmet Needs

*"Desire is better than despair;
determination is better than concern;
a plan is better than a dream—but only
action makes a difference."*

A Lesson Worth Copying

No one today can imagine a world without copy machines, yet even as recently as World War II no one could foresee what they could do. No one, that is, but Chester Carlson. An only child in a desperately poor family, he became fascinated with the technology of printing and decided early on to be an inventor. After putting himself through college and graduating in 1930 with a degree in physics, he worked at a series of jobs and spent his leisure hours in a home laboratory, experimenting with what would later become *xerography* (Greek for "dry writing").

Carlson filed his first patent in 1937, produced the first copy one year later, and spent the next six years trying to interest the business world in his invention. With war raging, corporations were putting their R&D money into the war effort. No one saw any pressing need for Carlson's invention.

Eventually he was able to convince a nonprofit agency in Ohio to work with him on developing a product, and in 1946 Haloid (later Xerox) rolled out the first machine. Fourteen years later, the Xerox 914 began its ubiquitous appearance in offices around the country.

"For every problem there is a solution that is simple, neat and wrong."
—H. L. Mencken, journalist, commentator

Encouraging Innovation

Have you ever come across someone else's brilliant idea, struck yourself on the forehead and wondered, "Why didn't I think of that?" Companies like McDonald's and Xerox Corporation have the resources to set up innovation centers where new ideas are incubated, but anyone can use their entrepreneurial tactics—for free. Here are a few:

~ **Combine ideas.** In creating new products or service offerings, be on the alert for intersections between one idea and another.

~ **Think backwards.** Begin with a product or service in mind and work backward, figuring out how the idea can become a practical reality in terms of cost and technology.

~ **Create an internal incubation fund.** Employees can be a great source of ideas, so set aside a budget for encouraging and testing out new concepts.

2. Leaders Possess an Irresistible Desire for Improvement

"Talent is only a starting point."
—Irving Berlin, composer

The Ultimate Patriot

Andrew Jackson, the seventh U.S. president, served as a messenger in the Revolutionary War when he was only a 13-year-old boy. As a young man, he became a major general in the Tennessee militia. During the War of 1812, he took 2,500 volunteer militiamen to Natchez, Mississippi and subsequently refused the Secretary of War's orders to abandon them there. Instead, Jackson paid for their supplies and marched them home. He later fought the British in New Orleans and Indians in Pensacola. He was guided by the words "One man with courage makes a majority."

"Luck is a dividend of sweat. The more you sweat, the luckier you get."

—Ray Kroc, founder, McDonald's

Good Wasn't Good Enough for Him

Seymour Cray became a revolutionary in the field of computer technology because he couldn't leave well-enough alone. In the late 1940s, he played a key role in developing one of the first business-oriented computers. Though he earned a reputation as a design genius, he felt he could do better on his own and in 1957 he and a partner launched Control Data Systems. They produced the first "supercomputer," then came up with a faster, more powerful model soon after. But the partner was reluctant to push even harder for improved machines, and a frustrated Cray left to form his own company, Cray Research.

Cray understood how bureaucracy could interfere with creativity. He protected his engineers from corporate red tape by moving them to remote offices, but he refused to micromanage them. And though he could have let others do the "grunt" work, he didn't; hands-on was his style.

In 1976, he unveiled the CRAY-1, which featured a vector processing technique that allowed for faster calculations. Its first customer, Los Alamos National Laboratory, bought the unit for $8.8 million. Nine years later, he introduced the even faster CRAY-2.

Before his death in a car accident in 1996, Cray had received awards for contributions to large-scale computer design and multiprocessor systems and patents for vector register technology, computer cooling systems and magnetic amplifiers.

"The starting point for all achievement is desire. Weak desires bring weak results, just as a small amount of fire makes a small amount of heat."
—Napoleon Hill, author

3. Leaders Are Willing to Sacrifice Leisure Time and Devote Effort and Energy to Learn

> *"Happiness and expertise go hand in hand. The better I am prepared, the happier I become."*

Sports and War

We use the term "natural athlete" to describe someone whose playing style appears effortless, but in sports—as in every other area of life—there is no achievement without effort. Ty Cobb, one of the five original National Baseball Hall of Fame inductees, had a .366 lifetime batting average, 4189 hits, 2245 runs and three .400 seasons in a 23-year major league career. To him, a fierce competitor, baseball was war and failure was not an option.

Baseball became a fascination for Cobb while he was in his teens and he lost no time preparing for a career as a professional player. He worked out on a local track, performing snap starts and running with his knees high-pumping. He'd fashion bats out of scraps of wood and go looking for pick-up games at local parks.

When he got to the majors, Cobb would warm up in the on-deck circle by twirling three bats around, so that when he came up to the plate, the single bat would feel lighter by comparison, and he'd have more control of his swing. He cultivated a belligerent, take-charge attitude so that pitchers would fear him. When he ran the bases, he ducked and dodged to avoid being hit by thrown balls, and he studied the fielders' body language so he could outmaneuver them.

Though he was known by some as the meanest man who ever played baseball, Cobb dedicated each game to his father, who died young and never had the chance to see him play, and he never missed an opportunity to perfect his craft.

"An investment in knowledge always pays the best interest."
—Ben Franklin, statesman, inventor

A Bronze Star for Avoiding Combat

In the military, the quality of leadership is frequently a matter of life or death. Army 1st Lt.

Matthew Cousins was deployed to Iraq in the early days of the war as part of a tactical team searching for chemical and biological weapons.

In each of the 70 missions he conducted across the desert, guiding nonmilitary specialists to inspection sites, he faced the threat of attack by rocket-propelled grenades, improvised explosive devices, mortar fire and insurgents on the ground.

"You always fear the unknown," Cousins said, "but as far as confidence in myself and willingness to serve, I was ready for it." In an attempt to take only the most secure routes, he and his team of non-commissioned officers studied maps and sat through nightly briefings on which areas were experiencing hostile fire. Sometimes they would scout a site first before bringing in the civilians. And they made sure to vary the times of the missions to keep the enemy off balance.

In all those missions, there was not a single incident or injury, and Cousins, who earned a Bronze Star for keeping his charges out of harm's way, credits their success to all of that detailed planning. As for his leadership abilities, he gives that credit to his father, Jack Cousins, a Vietnam vet whose work ethic was to stick with the job until the job is done.

Patrick Lee appears to be a leader in the making. The high school senior received the

Union League Club of Chicago's prestigious "Democracy in Action" award for bringing the Mikva Challenge to his suburban Chicago school. The service program, named for a former U. S. Congressman, is designed to involve students in elections and democracy. According to the nomination essay written by two of his teachers, Lee "revealed a depth of policy understanding and a passion for a democratic process."

The son of Korean immigrants, Lee has been an achiever all his young life. He has played the violin all over the world, is an all-state tennis player, and a class officer. He received perfect scores on the SAT and ACT.

Between studying, extracurricular activities, and going to awards banquets, Lee doesn't have time for television, but he relaxes occasionally by playing video games on the old Nintendo he got in grade school. "I take everything in stride and have a passion for all that I do," he says. "If that means I get an award, great. But I'm not going to change to win an award."

4. Leaders Accept Gradual Success to Gain Confidence Needed

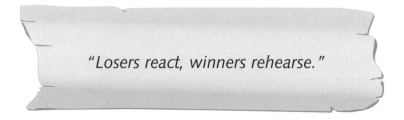

"Losers react, winners rehearse."

The Beauty of Persistence

Estee Lauder, named by Time Magazine as one of the 20 most influential builders and titans of the 20th century, began her cosmetic business in 1946 in the kitchen of her Manhattan home. She would mix the ingredients for her skin creams, lipsticks and eye shadows on her stove and then take them to beauty salons in her neighborhood and offer the women free samples. She could not afford conventional advertising. Whatever profits she made went into producing more free samples. If customers liked the product, they'd buy it on the spot.

Next she aimed for space on department store shelves, wooing buyers by personally inviting them to lunch on her elegant office terrace and demonstrating her products on them. As the stores expanded into other cities, she committed to appearing in person at every opening, and she stayed on to train the sales force.

When competition or economic downturns affected sales, she came up with better products and expanded into other lines. Against the advice of their lawyer and accountant, Lauder and her husband risked their life savings to grow the business, believing that no one can become a success without taking chances. Instead of the predicted financial ruin, the enterprise thrived. Today, annual sales are in the billions of dollars. According to Lauder, persistence is what makes a person successful. "It's that certain little spirit that compels you to stick it out just when you're at your most tired," she said. "It's that quality that forces you to find the route around the stone wall."

> *"The more tough lessons you learn early in life, the fewer errors you make later."*
> —Michael Steinhardt, investment manager

Chef Serves Up "No Excuses" Menu

Patrick O'Connell is chef of the world-famous Inn at Little Washington, whose dining room was ranked among America's best by Zagat's hotel survey. He shares his 5-course system for delivering the "perfect experience":

Assess the customer's mood. Their state of mind is critical to the experience they're about to have. At the Inn, the dining room captain rates each guest on a scale of 1-10, with 10 being happiest. The rating is shared with the entire staff so each person can make an effort to react. Their goal is for no one to leave the restaurant in a mood below 9.

Back courtesy with competence. To encourage learning and develop expertise, each employee is assigned a research project, which can range from exotic mushrooms to vintage wines. The employee presents a report to co-workers so that everyone can benefit. Dining room staffers have an additional assignment—to study restaurant reviews so they can cultivate an understanding of how opinion makers influence the marketplace.

Correct errors instantly. O'Connell compares the Inn dining experience with an artistic performance, and says that mistakes tarnish the show. By correcting them on the spot, the employee knows exactly what's expected, and bad habits are not allowed to form.

Hire people with the right attitude. Ability and experience are less important than attitude. "Nice people can be taught almost anything," O'Connell says. How do you find them? During the hiring process, ask about previous employers.

Applicants who have positive things to say tend to make better employees. **Forget how to say the word "no."** Staffers are also discouraged from saying "I don't know." Information about ingredients, preparation, and the Inn itself is conveyed in a monthly newsletter. A list of the 12 most-asked questions and how to answer them is also distributed.

> *"The more we know,*
> *the less we fear."*

5. Leaders Know What It Takes to Recover

> *"We learn 20% of what we know from victories and 80% from defeats."*

An Apprenticeship for Staying the Course

As a Navy pilot during World War II, former President George H.W. Bush was shot down twice in the Pacific theater, bailing out at 1,000 feet over open water. Later, as an entrepreneur in the booming oil business, he endured the failure of his first venture. When he got into politics, running for chairman of his county's Republican Party, he had to face down the powerful John Birch Society, an ultraconservative group that had no tolerance for any view but its own. Weeks of hard campaigning every night won him the position.

In his long political career Bush served as a U.S. congressman, a U.N. ambassador, and two terms as vice-president under Ronald Regan. Bush's greatest challenge came during his presidency, when Iraq invaded Kuwait in August 1990. Months of negotiations got the U.S. nowhere, and Bush resolved the following January to end the Gulf crisis by launching Operation Desert Storm. In six weeks, our troops defeated the Iraqis and liberated Kuwait.

"Lesson for Leaders: The best marksmen always take practice shots."

Weathering Failure

Joel Myers loved winds, clouds, rain, snow, and all sorts of temperatures, from scorching highs to frigid lows. Weather was his passion. He earned a doctorate in meteorology, but first-hand experience always appealed to him. Once, to gain an understanding of the force of an approaching hurricane, he fashioned a waist harness from a clothesline and attached himself to his front porch.

He launched AccuWeather Inc. in 1962 while he was still a grad student, and was the company's marketer, salesman and accountant in addition to being its sole forecaster. To get his first 100 customers, Myers had to make 25,000 cold calls. "That means I had 24,900 failures," he said. "I was relentless and driven."

Myers used his predicting abilities to make wise investment decisions in the commodities market, where weather events affect crop prices.

AccuWeather grew to become the world's largest commercial weather forecasting organization, with over 60,000 paid customers, 85 forecasters, and 34 data-collecting satellite dishes. Myers was named by *Entrepreneur* magazine as one of the 500 greatest entrepreneurs in the history of the U.S. A colleague of his once said, "Joel really insists on succeeding. He doesn't accept the word 'try.'"

How Not To Perish

Every year, some 300,000 businesses are launched in the U.S., but 4 out of every 5 will fail. In, *Be the Elephant: Build a Bigger, Better Business*, author Steve Kaplan offers this advice on how to grow your business. His thesis is that businesses that do not evolve will deteriorate over time.

Conduct a dollars-and-cents analysis of your business model. Without numbers, "business is just expensive gambling," Kaplan says. That's why owners need a solid idea of expenses compared to projected income. There are only two ways to make money: increase sales and decrease costs.

Decide where new business will come from and how you will handle it. Is it better for you to sell new customers existing products or to sell existing customers new products? Will you need to form strategic alliances or can you handle the increase in business internally? Your sales force can help you develop this information.

Be a hands-on leader. It takes as much as a year or two to develop managers who really understand the business.

2

Winners and Leaders Are Ready

The Undertow of Life

All surfers study the crests of breaking waves and the undertow of currents. Riding the "tube" created by breakers is their exhilarating challenge. Being caught in an undertow can be a life-threatening hazard.

Escaping the undertow dangers is a problem for all of us because:

~ We naively believe we are immune from danger

~ The signals of conditions which will pull us under are usually not obvious

~ We are not disciplined enough to stay out of the water when it is dangerous

~ We have not studied escape options

~ We have not determined where and how to get help

Because the dangers of "undertow" factors in our lives are not likely to ever disappear completely, we must always give thought to our options. If we don't prepare we have only one alternative—sink.

We are ready for more responsibility if:

We start wherever we are.

"Your organization will never get better unless you are willing to admit that there is something wrong with it."

— Norman Schwarzkopf, U.S. Army General

The 10 Commandments for Advancement

1. Thou shalt not confuse dreams with reality.
2. Thou shalt not blindly accept opinions over facts.
3. Thou shalt learn to be accountable.
4. Thou shalt invest in thyself.
5. Thou shalt first test ideas for usefulness.
6. Thou shalt live below thy means.
7. Thou shalt focus on results vs. activities.
8. Thou shalt not be influenced by excuse-makers.
9. Thou shalt support calculated risk-taking.
10. Thou shalt promise only what is deliverable.

"Beware those who always seek comfort and avoid risk; they are likely to wilt when trouble comes."

From Rags to Riches

In 1976, Steve Jobs and Steve Wozniak raised $1,350 in seed capital by selling a VW van and their Hewlett-Packard programmable calculator. Then they built the first Apple PC in Job's garage.

Black & Decker was launched in 1910 for $1,200. Six years later the founders realized there was greater demand for their electric drills than for their other products and changed direction. Today the company is a $5 billion enterprise.

Ernest and Julio Gallo invested $923 of their own money and borrowed another $5,000 to launch their winery. They knew nothing about wine-making, but they learned by studying books from their local library.

Hewlett-Packard got its start during the Great Depression with an investment of $538. Its first big client was Walt Disney, who needed sound production equipment for his animated film, "Fantasia."

Marriott International began as a nine-seat

A&W soda fountain, launched by Bill Marriott and two others with $3,000 and a knack for drawing a crowd. On their first day of business, May 20, 1927, they played a radio that kept patrons clued in to Lindbergh's progress on his first trans-Atlantic flight.

In 1907 two teens launched a delivery service for merchants with $100 of pooled money. A hundred years later, we know that company as United Parcel Service.

"The 80/20 rule applies to the process of making significant changes. 80% of the time new leadership will be required."

Staying Ahead of Changing Times

Ted Bensinger was the new head of Brunswick Corp., the country's top seller of bowling equipment, when rival American Machine & Foundry came out with the first automatic pin setting device in 1952. Brunswick had put off developing its own automatic pinsetters because of the steep costs of R&D, and by the time it did, AMF had placed its units in 9,000 lanes across the country.

Brunswick had been founded as a carriage-building company in 1845 by Bensinger's great grandfather, John Brunswick. Staying ahead of changing times had been a tradition. Carriages became obsolete when cars replaced them, so Brunswick went into the manufacture of saloon fixtures. When those products became unprofitable during the days of Prohibition, the company turned to luxury gaming items such as pool tables, which lost favor during the Depression. The business had managed to survive for over 100 years by embracing change but, in the case of the automatic pinsetters, it was apparent that Brunswick had dropped the ball.

It would be another four years before its model was ready. Bensinger went after the market aggressively, dubbing his machines "Worth Waiting For." Faster and more reliable than AMF's device, it was in 11,000 lanes by 1958, two years after its introduction. Helping to achieve this feat was the offer the company made to lane owners, who could buy the $8,000 machines for a little as 10 percent down and take eight years to pay them off.

In 1954, before the introduction of its automatic pinsetters, Brunswick's sales were $33 million. Sales grew to $422 million by 1961.

Keeping Cool When Business Gets Hot

Beyond Fleece, Scott Jones' custom jacket manufacturing company was experiencing astounding
growth during its fifth year of operation. Though
Jones had no employees, operating expenses kept
eating into profits, and he couldn't afford to hire a
consultant. Jones did take the free advice offered
by retired business executives, who encouraged
him to apply for a loan from the Small Business
Administration. He used most of the $30,000 he
received to enhance his web site—a vital move
since his business model bypassed retailers and
sold directly to the public.

Shortly thereafter, the company received a positive review in Backpacker magazine—a staffer
had bought one of its products—and that expo-
sure led to a surge of orders. With the increased
cash flow, Jones hired a few workers and expanded his line.

Jones, who received the SBA's Young Entrepreneur of the year Award, now employs a dozen
workers and has a 2,500 square-foot facility for
manufacturing and warehousing. He offers this
advice for anyone staring out: "Do something
you're passionate about—a business or service
you love doing—and you'll be successful."

"If you never see me at my best, you never know what I can do."

An Elite Force

After Army Major Charles Beckwith spent a year training with the British Special Air Service (SAS) during the Vietnam war, he realized the U.S. needed a similar elite unit. Although his recommendation was met with no enthusiasm from the Pentagon, that setback did not deter him. He simply switched tactics, put his report in an envelope, and mailed it to his state senator. The senator placed a call to Army headquarters to inquire about the project, and that set things in motion.

Delta Force is one of America's secret weapons, though it doesn't officially exist. Its members are sent on the most dangerous missions to collect intelligence. Beckwith's vision was to find the best men, set exacting standards, and train for every possible contingency by mastering a variety of skills: drive a locomotive or an 18 wheeler, repair an elevator, read a blueprint, pick a lock. They spend hours every day shooting handguns and submachine guns. Snipers must be able to hit every target at 600 yards and 90% of their targets at 1,000 yards. They are considered the best marksmen in the world.

Continual self-improvement is imperative, and Beckwith held think-tank meetings every week to encourage fresh ideas.

We are Disciplined to Keep Going

> *"For winners, defeat is temporary . . .*
> *and so is success."*

World Wild Web

Even before they could figure out how their enterprise would make its first dollar, Yahoo! founders David Filo and Jerry Yang considered themselves among the luckiest people in the world. The two were working 20-hour days in an effort to bring order to the once-chaotic World Wide Web and, because in 1994 the Internet was fast becoming the next big thing, they were loving it.

Well, for the most part they were. "It was tough," said Yang. "We really didn't know which business model would work, and we considered everything."

They kept at it, believing that the internet could change people's lives. They were right.

> *"Mistakes are the portals of discovery."*
> —James Joyce, writer

Lemonade from Lemons

Life for Anna Bradley was hard and getting harder. A third major health crisis had forced the then-35-year-old IT executive to give up her job, move into to her parents' home and join the ranks of the disabled. But she was used to working and couldn't imagine living as an invalid. Aggressive and curious by nature, she continued to look for opportunities.

While researching amendments to the "Disability Act," Bradley discovered that anyone doing business with the federal government had to make their technology accessible to people with disabilities. People who are deaf, blind, visually impaired or who must work their keyboards with a mouth-held stick use special software to help them surf the Internet and navigate web sites. Section 508 of the "Disability Act" requires Web sites to support software for users with disabilities. This gave her the idea for a new business.

Her company, Criterion 508 Solutions, has worked with FEMA, the IRS, the National Institutes of Health and a number of state universities as well as private sector clients that include Hewlett-Packard and Citibank. Jobs run from $12,000 to over $100,000.

Bradley's vision wasn't just to help businesses and agencies comply with the new legislation. She also wanted to create job opportunities for others with disabilities. "Guess what," she says, "they've got a skill set, which is their disability, which you can't go to college to learn." About half of her 30 employees have a serious disability such as blindness and cerebral palsy.

Future Confidence is
Based Upon Past Success

"Ferocity is typically fake. The quiet ones usually win in the end."

Born To Run

Grete Waitz lived her life at top speed—literally. As a child in Norway, she'd race alongside buses and run 6:30-minute miles with her brother. She became the Norwegian junior champion in the 400 and 800 meters at age 16.

Her energy and determination weren't always enough. In 1971, she competed unsuccessfully in the European Championships, and in 1976 she failed to win a medal at the Montreal Olympics. Discouraged but not defeated, she decided to cut back on her running for a time, and instead competed in cross-country skiing and team handball. The following year, refreshed in body and spirit, she returned her focus to running and took the gold medal in the World Cup 3,000-meter race.

By this time, Waitz had a career as a school teacher, but she still trained diligently morning and evening, getting up before dawn and running in every kind of weather. "If the training isn't tough enough," she said, "it won't work."

Her husband thought she should take on a bigger challenge, the 1978 New York City Marathon. No one expected her to win—including Waitz herself—but she did, setting a world record of 2:32:30, which she broke two years later at 2:27:33.

"Inspiration is not instinctive. It comes only to those who think and learn to incubate options."

An Offer He Could Refuse

When prominent Chicago architect David Burnham offered the up-and-coming Frank Lloyd Wright the opportunity to study at the École des Beaux-Arts in Paris, Wright turned him down. The offer included another two years at the American Academy in Rome and full financial support for Wright's wife and six children, but the young man had other ideas. He viewed the classical tradition as an impediment to creativity. "I'd rather be free and a failure," he said as he prepared to experiment with new technologies, which included plate glass windows and suspended toilet bowls. A believer in organic design, he felt that buildings needed to grow naturally from their surroundings. One of Wright's most famous buildings, *Fallingwater*, was named "Building of the 20th Century" by the American Institute of Architects.

Looking Backward for Direction

The corporate vision of pharmaceutical giant Merck & Co. had always been to preserve and improve human life. It developed the first penicillin in the U.S., chemotherapy in the 1930s and 1940s, and was the first drug company to establish its own research laboratories.

It faced a dilemma in the 1980s, trying to decide whether to invest the time and resources to find a cure for a gruesome disease known as river blindness, which afflicts people in Third World countries, or to move on to more profitable projects. They decided to pursue the cure for river blindness, but when the drug *Mectizan* was developed, no aid organization or government agency was interested in purchasing it.

Merck then announced that it would give the drug away and create a foundation so that the people who needed it would get it. Not only would that validate the efforts of the scientists who had worked on the drug, it would keep the company true to its mission to relieve human suffering.

When, Where and How to Change

"Definition of insanity: Repetition, expecting the outcome will be different."

A Necessary Shift in Focus

McDonald's Corp. had always relied on a single strategy to achieve its phenomenal rate of growth—build hundreds of new stores every year. That strategy had served the company well for four decades, but by 2003, sales were lagging. It was up to the newly appointed CEO, Charlie Bell, to engineer a turnaround.

Bell had been a McDonald's employee all his working life, beginning in his teens as a part-time crew member cleaning restrooms at a unit in Sydney. Four years later, he had become Australia's youngest store manager. He was in his early forties when he was tapped to head the company, and he brought to his role years of experience running operations in Australia, Asia and Europe, plus a flair for marketing and a willingness to take chances.

Sales began to rebound quickly once Bell's plan was put into place. The focus shifted away from new store openings and toward improvements in existing restaurants. Units were renovated, customers were given new menu options such as breakfast items and salads, and the "I'm Lovin' It" advertising campaign was launched.

Only a month after taking the helm at McDonald's, Bell was diagnosed with cancer, and he died of the disease less than a year later at age 44. Company executives believe that the simple strategic shift he helped engineer will have a lasting impact.

Finding the Right Niche

When achievement does not bring happiness, perhaps it's time for something different. Michael Crocker had become a successful human resources executive, but he had lost his enthusiasm for the career path he was on and, encouraged by family and friends, decided to go back to school to become an engineer.

He entered the Cisco Networking Academy Program at Tidewater Community College in Virginia. After graduation, he landed a job with Multimax, an IT support company that works with the government and the military.

Crocker was assigned to work on the Navy/Marine Corps Intranet—with over 500,000 daily users, the NMCI is the second largest network in the world—and continued his education. "Technology changes so quickly, you don't want to be left behind," he said. Taking advantage of his employer's tuition reimbursement program, he went for certification as an Internet expert. After passing the written portion of the certification exam, he received a promotion on the NMCI project. He is now a senior network engineer. Best of all, Crocker says, "I enjoy my job; I like going to work. Very few people can say that."

"A misled individual is deceived. A misled army is massacred."

Stumbling but Not Falling

There have been a few missteps in the history of athletic shoe manufacturer Nike. Founder Phil Knight launched the company in 1964 intending to manufacture inexpensive running shoes that would compete with pricey Adidas; he grew it into a worldwide sports apparel business with annual sales of $15 billion.

But along the way Knight failed to anticipate the aerobics craze of the 1980s, nor did he figure that he would some day have to cater to the tastes of women and the particular shapes of their feet. (Reebok, the new guys on the block, took the lead there.) More recently, Nike was heavily criticized for paying barely subsistence wages to workers at some of its plants in Asia. In 2000, he had a falling out with the University of Oregon, his alma mater, after it joined the Workers Rights Consortium.

The stumble in the 1980s included two consecutive quarterly losses, and Knight realized that he would have to come up with new designs to win back market share. Nike introduced air-pumped cross-trainers in its now-legendary ad campaign featuring two-sport champion Bo Jackson. A decade later, reacting quickly to the charges of sub-standard wages and working conditions, Knight ordered its Asian factories to increase wages and improve standards. His relationship with the university repaired, Knight has since become its largest single donor.

3

If You're Not Ready Now—When?

> *"To delay until all conditions are perfect is to forfeit the game."*

Those who are successful over time have learned how to put themselves in a continuing state of readiness. They are anxious to make change work for them. They probe for new ways to solve old problems and need the satisfaction of converting doubters to their views and contentions.

The Boy Scout motto says it all: *Be Prepared.* But repeating it is not enough. It can become a mindset when we understand these basic principles:

1. Stop Wishing and Start Working
2. Create Your Own Luck
3. Associate with People Who Are Prepared
4. Expand Core Talents
5. Expect Continuous Improvement
6. Don't Back Away from Problems
7. Stick to It

Stop Wishing and Start Working

The door to her dream of becoming a priest slammed shut for Sister Rose Marie Lorentzen on a day in 1979 when Pope John Paul made it clear that women should not expect to take on that role in the Church. The news made her profoundly angry and sad, but it didn't deter her from her life's work: to help the helpless. She turned her anger into action by founding the Chicago area's first temporary housing system for the homeless. It has since become a model for the nation.

Public Action to Deliver Shelter (PADS) now serves thousands of people in hundreds of communities, but in those early years, Sister Rose Marie waged an aggressive uphill battle with community leaders, who either denied homelessness existed or were unwilling to have shelters established in their backyards. She wrote letters to newspapers about the problem, and lobbied in Springfield for legislation to allow homeless children to stay in their home school districts. She opencd Hesed House in a brick building in downtown Aurora, IL, which is now a center offering emergency shelter, transitional apartments and support services in addition to a food pantry, clothes closet, and medical and legal aid clinics.

One former shelter resident, now a chemical engineering student, said she changed his life by "making me realize there's nothing you can't do until you try it."

Create Your Own Luck

Seinfeld may have been a mega-hit whose characters will live in reruns forever, but Jack Benny's 1950-1965 TV series was the original show about "nothing." Benny's genius lay in his ability to master the details. Though he had no forerunners to copy, his innovations were often the result of learning from mistakes other comedians made. He knew that timing was less about speech and more about knowing when to pause, and on his popular radio show, he tailored every joke to make sure listeners could visualize each nuance and move.

In 1931, the year before his radio show began, Benny was just another struggling comedian, when he was invited to appear on Ed Sullivan's local radio show in New York. Sullivan was a journalist who interviewed entertainers. Instead of going on the air to chat, Benny decided to make his own luck, and he came prepared with a five-minute string of jokes. The reaction was electric. Soon sponsors had given Benny his own series. The radio show ran for 23 years.

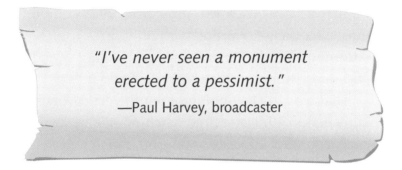

"I've never seen a monument erected to a pessimist."
—Paul Harvey, broadcaster

Was it luck or planning that led Col. James Hickey and the soldiers of the 4th Infantry Division's 1st Brigade to capture former Iraqi dictator Saddam Hussein on December 13, 2003? They had been working on locating him since the previous summer and had staged a dozen previous raids. Operating in such a volatile area meant that the soldiers had to be prepared for whatever reaction the enemy threw at them, but Hickey said he had a strong prior feeling the raid that night was going to be a good one. "Just for a millisecond, I had an enormous sense of accomplishment. I was very, very happy we got that job done."

Associate with People
Who Are Prepared

It was a simple business plan that Rollin King sketched out on a cocktail napkin, with the words "Dallas," "San Antonio" and "Houston" written in each corner. An airline with only three routes? Attorney Herb Kelleher turned to his pilot friend and said, "Rollin, you're crazy. Let's do it."

That was the beginning of Southwest Airlines, launched in 1971 at a time when no one believed such a concept could ever take off, much less succeed. But King and Kelleher were not only mavericks, they were mavericks who thought alike. They eliminated assigned seating and airline meals, offering passengers peanuts instead, and used the savings in money and manpower to reduce air fares to the point that they could compete with bus fares. Flight attendants were encouraged to crack jokes while they recited the emergency instructions. Later, Southwest became the first major airline to put up a web site and offer bookings online.

Here was a company that succeeded by breaking all the rules, but Kelleher believes it's the employees that have made all the difference. "Competitors have tried and failed to copy us because they cannot copy our people," he says. His method is as elegantly simple as King's business plan: find exceptional people, treat them with respect, and empower and encourage them to do their jobs better than even they thought possible.

> *"Setting a goal is not the main thing. It is deciding how you will go about achieving it and staying with that plan."*
> —Tom Landry, Superbowl coach

Expand Core Talents

Johannes Brahms is renowned as one of the great "three B's" of classical music, but he spent a good part of his career listening to critics carp about his serious tone and long compositional style. In Leipzig once, at a recital of his "Piano Concerto in D Minor," the audience hissed. Brahms was a native son of Hamburg, having grown up in the slums of that city, but its musical establishment routinely passed him over for the post of musical director of the Hamburg orchestra.

Though it might have been easier and more lucrative for him to go with the flow, Brahms continued to write and play his own style of music, always staying focused on his goal to become a great composer. He took inspiration from the works of other great composers and wrote variations on the music of Handel, Haydn, Paganini and Schumann. He had a great sensitivity to nature and kept a notebook to jot down ideas and impressions for later reference. He delighted in thunderstorms, which he said were gorgeous.

Eventually, Brahms got the recognition he deserved as audiences grew and the critics retreated. His variations, the endless reshaping of a basic melody, brought the form to its most advanced state in the 19th century. In the later years of his life, cities across Europe held grand festivals devoted exclusively to his works.

Terry Beauvais took early retirement from the Postal Service and spent her new free time making jewelry. She had never been a businesswoman during her working life, but her hobby was getting expensive, and so she decided to sell some of her wares at local arts and crafts shows. She took a class to learn how to make her own beads, then launched Blue-Jean Beads with only $200 in startup costs for equipment and materials.

Meeting customers face to face helped Beauvais build her sales technique, and talking with other vendors added to her store of business acumen. Less than two years after starting her company, she was able to average $1,000 a day in sales at the shows.

Expect Continuous Improvement

Before Bill Bowerman co-founded Nike, Inc., he was the head track and field coach at the University of Oregon, and he was fascinated with physiology and the dynamics of running. In the late 1950s, runners were still wearing shoes that were too cumbersome to be efficient. Bowerman estimated that 200 cumulative pounds could be lifted from a runner during a one-mile race for every ounce removed from a shoe's weight. He devised an athletic shoe with a lighter sole, a heel wedge and better support.

Unable to find anyone who would manufacture such a shoe, he decided to do it himself, tinkering constantly and using team members to test his designs. In 1964, he and former team member Phil Knight founded Blue Ribbon Sports to sell their designs to others.

As a coach Bowerman was one of the greatest, with an impressive championship record and a reputation for encouraging his athletes to reach for their maximum potential. As an innovator, he never stopped aiming for the perfect running shoe. It was while eating breakfast one morning in 1971 that he hit on the idea for a shoe with a sole patterned like a waffle. It became the Nike brand, which he and Knight launched the next year. That year, of the top seven finishers in the Olympic marathon, four were wearing Nikes.

The company changed its name to Nike, Inc. in 1980 and went public. Bowerman believed that to stay ahead, the company had to keep improving. Today it has grown into the world's largest sports and fitness enterprise whose products are marketed in over 100 countries.

> *"My wife and I were happy for 20 years. Then we met."*
> —Rodney Dangerfield, comedian

Don't Back Away from Problems

The father of the microwave oven, Percy Spencer, kept going when others might have given up. Orphaned at the age of three, he was raised by an impoverished widowed aunt, and had to drop out of school after the seventh grade to take a job as an apprentice machinist. His fascination with technology began when his plant was wired for electricity. Then he heard about wireless telegraphic communications and joined the Navy to learn more. When he left the military, he joined a company that developed wireless telegraphic systems, but that company went bankrupt.

By this time Spencer had gained enough

practical hands-on experience to put him ahead of the scientific theorists. In 1925, he was hired by Raytheon, which was then a small electronics upstart. He joined a team of engineers who were adapting rectifier tubes to convert analog signals into digital ones. As radios became more powerful, engineers were challenged to improve these tubes so they would stand up under higher voltages. After many failures, Spencer was the only engineer to come up with a solution. The new tube not only saved the company, it led to a threefold increase in sales.

At the start of World War II, Spencer developed magnetron tubes for the transmission of microwave signals that would allow planes and ships to make and receive messages. Raytheon began mass production of the tubes but orders barely trickled in. Spencer came up with innovations to increase production from 17 a week to 2600 a day, and the military took notice.

Raytheon produced more than 75 percent of all magnetron tubes used by the Allied Forces, but as the war wound down, demand dropped. Again Raytheon was in trouble and again Spencer came to the rescue, this time with microwaves. He had begun tinkering with them after he noticed that a piece of chocolate melted in the presence of a tube he was testing.

He filed his first patent for the microwave oven two months after the end of the war, but it was twenty years before they came into general commercial use.

Stick to It

James Fergason invented the first practical application of liquid crystal and discovered the properties of crystals that made LCD technology possible. He holds more than 130 U.S. patents and over 500 foreign patents. In 2006 he received the $500,000 Lemelson-MIT Prize, the largest cash prize given in the U.S. for invention.

"I love looking at something and coming up with something that somebody else missed," he says of his years of researching, but it's his stubbornness that he credits for his accomplishments. This is what he believes it takes to "stick to it:"

- Be interested enough in your project to keep at it.
- Move forward, no matter what the reverses are.
- Avoid falling in love with your ideas. You should be able to admit when you're going in the wrong direction.
- Look at all sides of a problem so you can come at something from a new angle.
- Ignore everyday stresses, and keep events in perspective. Nothing is worth a heart attack.

*"There is no success without
difficult decisions."*

Norwegian archeologist and explorer Thor Heyerdahl risked his life to prove that Indians from South America were the first to settle the Polynesian Islands. Academics had always insisted that the first inhabitants of the islands had to have come from Asia, since ancient rafts could not hold up for 4,000 miles.

In 1947, Heyerdahl built the *Kon-Tiki,* a 45-ft. raft made of balsa wood tied together with ropes, the only materials used by ancient people, and set sail across the Pacific. One hundred and one days later he and five companions reached their destination. Though scientists remained unimpressed by his achievement, his book about the experience was a best-seller, and his documentary won an Academy Award.

Two decades later, Heyerdahl set out to cross the Atlantic from Morocco in a reed boat. He wanted to prove a link between ancient Egyptians and Central and South America. His first reed boat, the *Ra,* had to be abandoned after it took on water, but he completed the voyage 10 months later, reaching the West Indies in 57 days.

"Expecting recognition for a good deed diminishes its significance."

As vice-president of Chevron's global refining and marketing business, Patricia Woertz was one of the most powerful women in the male-dominated oil industry. She had risen up the ranks quickly and was in charge of an operation with 30,000 employees in 180 countries and annual revenues of $100 billion., but when she realized it might take her another four or five years to become CEO, she resigned without a backward glance, even though she had no idea where her next paycheck would come from.

Woertz had always placed a high value on honest communication and that decision freed her to pursue other CEO opportunities full time and be entirely candid abut what she wanted. Three months later, she was hired as the new chief executive of Archer Daniels Midland, an agricultural powerhouse based in Decatur, Illinois.

In an interview, Woertz once said that she'd never had a job held by a woman before her, but she has never considered gender a factor in her career. A vice president at Chevron once remarked, "It's been apparent for as long as I've

known her that she had high aspirations. That's
one of the reasons I respected her so much."

> *"There is no security on this earth;
> there is only opportunity."*
> —Douglas MacArthur, U.S. Army General

4

The Best Time to Deliver

> *"Initiative and perseverance are brothers who win. Delay and idleness are brothers who lose."*

The worst mistake is to assume change will favor you. The best plan to yield positive results is to prepare. The best time to deliver is now.

These 8 tasks will enable you to objectively evaluate your readiness:

1. Don't Wait Too Long

John Sperling is the founder of the University of Phoenix. It is owned by a publicly traded holding company he heads. His is a rags-to-mega-riches story that could easily have ended when he, a dyslexic former merchant marine, earned a Ph.D. from Cambridge University and became a history professor at a state university. The quiet life of an academic, even with all the comforts of tenure, wasn't for him, though he didn't realize that until many years later.

An ex-trade unionist and a radical by nature, Sperling had risen to a national leadership position in the American Federation of Teachers. He went on to form the United Professors of California and led the union in what turned out to be a disastrous month-long strike during which 100 professors came close to losing their jobs in a mass firing.

"The strike was one of the most liberating experiences of my life," Sperling said. It taught him to insulate himself from criticism. That psychological immunity got him through the hostility and legal assaults of the higher-education establishment as he was establishing his radically different "distance learning" system. The University of Phoenix aims to provide working adults with real-world knowledge. Its curriculum is built around learning groups headed by professionals who teach at night what they work at by day. Sperling fought for years to gain accreditation, and received it in 1979. The University of Phoenix is today the largest for-profit university system in the world.

Timing may be everything, as the old saying

goes, but waiting and hoping for the exact right time to launch an enterprise is self-defeating. "Are these crazy times?" asks business writer Seth Godin. "You bet they are. But so were the days when we were doing duck-and-cover air-raid drills in school, or going through the scares of Three Mile Island and Love Canal."

He points out that on the flip side of economic downturns, of crises at home and abroad, opportunities arise that we have an obligation to pursue. For example, an American startup company manufactures an inexpensive irrigation device that it sells in Africa to help farmers triple their yields and move from subsistence to surplus. We must "find ideas that matter and share them," Godin says, "take risks and make the world better by being amazing."

"Delay is self-imposed paralysis."

2. Accept New Assignments

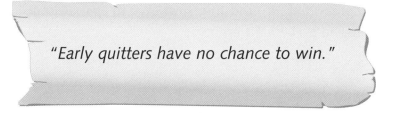

"Early quitters have no chance to win."

Steven Covey, best known for his 1989 book *The 7 Habits of Highly Effective People,* didn't set off in the direction of business self-help publishing until he was 50 years old. Up until then, he had been teaching organizational behavior at Brigham Young University. *7 Habits* encourages readers who want to be more effective to:

~ take the initiative
~ begin a project with a vision of how it will turn out
~ put first things first; be willing to sacrifice for the future
~ think win-win
~ listen more, speak less
~ understand the power of synergy
~ improve yourself in body, mind and spirit

7 Habits launched Covey into a new and extraordinarily successful career as an author and public speaker. The book sold upwards of 15 million copies worldwide in its first few years in print and continues to sell thousands of copies every month. In his follow-up book, *The 8th Habit*, Covey urges readers to find their voices and inspire others to find theirs, to give in to that longing to make a difference.

> "A current situation does not determine your future but it can be the starting point for what you will make happen."

Perfectionism, usually considered a positive attribute, becomes self-defeating when it stands in the way of action. Take the case of Vickie Milazzo, founder and president of a Houston firm that certifies legal nurse consultants. She estimated a three month timeline for a project that would result in the revision of her core product, a home-study seminar, but because of her overwhelming desire to get things "exactly right"—to keep tweaking the design and content of the seminar—the project took nearly three times as long to complete.

"I knew I needed to ditch my perfectionism," Milazzo says, adding that the company's position as the industry leader could easily have been compromised by a competitor during those long months of delay. To stifle her perfectionist urges, she focuses on separating vital issues from those clients probably won't even notice. Instead of working on *constant* modifications of an existing product, she notes major changes she wants to make and saves them for review at the proper time.

Milazzo says that by continuing to perfect something small, you may block bigger results. Now, before she commits precious resources, she asks two key questions: "Could we improve anything else here?" and "Do we have to make it better?"

> *"The 3 best words to build confidence are Stand And Deliver."*

3. Challenge Unsupported Opinions

Very often, the more a person does, the more he is capable of doing. As a child, Bob Mathias never pictured himself an athlete. It was only on a dare that he ran up to and cleared a four-foot hurdle at his brother's school. A gym teacher, impressed by his performance, offered to coach the frail 10 year old, who was still recovering from anemia.

Suddenly motivated, Mathias built himself up by diligently following his doctor's dietary instructions, scheduling more sleep, and focusing his limited energies on football, basketball and track. By the end of his sophomore year in high school, he had not only overcome his anemia, he had become an excellent athlete. He spent the summer lifting 100-lb. bags of sulfur into a crop-dusting plane and worked out in a backyard gym so he could improve his physique.

By his junior year, Mathias had mastered the discus and the hurdles, and when the team's high jumper got injured, he practiced the high jump until he could clear 5 feet 6 inches. At a meet shortly thereafter, he cleared a 5 ft. 10 inch hurdle to lead his team to victory. His coach suggested that Mathias might be a natural for the decathlon.

Mathias had to question other athletes to see what would be required for a decathlon, which consists of the 100-meter dash, long jump, shot put, high jump, 400-meter run, 110-meter hurdles, discus, pole vault, javelin and 1,500-meter run. His interest sparked, Mathias told his coach he was ready to get to work.

After he won a regional competition, beating out college athletes with his high scores, he tried out for and made the 1948 U.S. Olympic team. Mathias became the youngest American ever to win in track and field, and he was the only American to win the decathlon twice.

> *"Those who lack discipline will also lack courage."*

Two years after retiring from a spectacular 14-year NFL career, former running back Emmitt Smith was once again pumped for competition. This time it wasn't on the football field, but on the dance floor set of the ABC hit show "Dancing with the Stars." No one expected that he, a beefy 5 ft. 9 inch powerhouse, would take home a trophy for ballroom, but he did.

"I've defied the odds all my life," Smith said. He wasn't expected to be productive as a Dallas Cowboys running back for at least a dozen seasons, but he scored 100 touchdowns in only six seasons. In college at the University of Florida, he was named 1987 National Freshman Player of the Year and the 1989 Southeastern Conference Player of the Year.

According to Smith, a love for competition and the thrill of opportunity have always been his motivations. "I've always been somewhat of a person that has said, 'Man, I wonder, can I get that done?'"

4. Modify Previous Attempts

Without Jack Kilby's invention, the integrated circuit, we would have among other things no computers, no Internet, no space program and no digital watches. It took him about a day to put together a prototype on a slice of germanium the size of a paperclip. He demonstrated the circuit for management of the company he was working for, Texas Instruments, and the device was publicly unveiled six months later on March 6, 1959.

Meanwhile, Robert Noyce was working on a similar device for his employer, Fairchild Semiconductor. Noyce used silicon instead of germanium, which would prevent potential manufacturing problems inherent in Kilby's design. Noyce received his patent six months after Kilby was granted his.

The patents, which differed from each other only slightly, threatened to set off legal battles, until Noyce and Kilby—with the blessing of their respective employers—decided to become co-inventors and share royalties. Kilby received the Nobel Prize in 2000. Noyce became a co-founder of Intel.

"Time changes nothing for those who won't change themselves."

Connecting Main Street with Wall Street—that is, putting out business news that any Ordinary Joe can understand—is Neil Cavuto's passion. The highly opinionated host of Fox News Channel's "Your World" has no patience for elitists, academics, and jargon of any kind. He's more interested in the big picture than in the details of the Dow. And he admits he wants to push people to the edge, to elicit a reaction.

But to err is human, and Cavuto says he may have crossed the line many times. "I'll be the first to admit that there are shows we do where I shake my head and say, 'That didn't work.'"

5. Overcome Emotional Resistance

> *"Never let the fear of striking out get in your way."*
> —Babe Ruth, Baseball Legend

Up until his teenage years, Jack LaLanne was a weak and sickly child. His eating habits were poor, he filled up on all kinds of sweets, and he seldom spent any time playing outdoors. One day his neighbor told him about a man who was giving a lecture in a nearby town. The man was a crusading nutritionist and had helped many people regain their health, and young Jack decided to go and hear him speak.

LaLanne recalls how the man pounded up and down the stage, electrifying his audience as he exhorted them to eat only natural, unprocessed foods. "He had all this energy I wanted. I actually got down on my knees and said, 'Dear God, give me the willpower to refrain from eating these foods that are killing me!'"

His prayer was apparently successful. After building up his weak body, LaLanne joined his high school football team and later entered body-building competitions. During the Great Depression, he started his own gym, which included a health food store and juice bar. In the early 1950s, he became a pioneer in the fitness movement, bringing his message into people's homes and getting them to exercise in front of their TVs. Even into his 90s, LaLanne was still working out two hours a day. "It's an ego thing," he once said. "I just want to see how long I can keep this up."

"When temper flares, judgment burns."

6. Question Weak Evidence

> "Beware those who try to convince
> you about things they do not
> understand themselves."

To help his family pay its bills, Paul "Red" Adair dropped out of school during the Great Depression and worked at a number of dead-end jobs. He was an expert on exactly nothing until he landed a position with Otis Pressure Control, a company that dealt with gas field blowouts and fires. One December day in 1940, a blowout in an Arkansas gas well created a deafening roar that sent everyone running. Everyone, that is, but Adair, who remained calm so that he could evaluate the situation.

A flange on the mechanism that should have prevented the blowout had come loose. Adair knew that any resulting explosion would be deadly. Grabbing a long wrench and dodging the escaping gas, he managed to tighten the flange and avert a catastrophe.

That kind of daring served him well as an Army staff sergeant in the bomb disposal squadron during World War II, and later in his work in oil well fire and blowout control. He started his own company in 1959, and by the time of his death at age 89 in 2004, he and his crews had extinguished nearly 2,000 oil well fires and natural gas blowouts around the world, including the hundreds of fires set by a retreating Iraqi army during the 1991 Gulf War. Three U.S. presidents sent Adair official letters recognizing his courage and dedication.

Dr. Armand Hammer, a former chairman of Occidental Petroleum Company said once about Adair, "He's a man who absolutely understands his work."

> *"The best evidence of what you know is whether others understand what you say and do."*

The conventional wisdom is that you can't fight City Hall and you shouldn't mess with the Powers-That-Be.

7. Test Different Options

> *"Only a small part of wisdom*
> *comes from contemplation.*
> *Most results from hands-on work."*

At Walker Digital, the Connecticut company behind Priceline.com, new employees are given a
Rubik's Cube to keep on their desks. The six-
sided puzzle, which is completed when the small
squares are aligned so that each side displays a
solid block of color, is a reminder to examine all
sides of a problem before you try to solve it. According to company founder Jay Walker, if you
can't find at least six sides to a problem, you're
not looking hard enough and you're missing opportunities for breakthroughs.

Online travel reservations is Priceline's niche
and problem solving is at the heart of the business he founded in 1995. Walker knew that con-
sumers wanted to pay less for airline travel but,
given the system, had no way to indicate what
they would be willing to trade off in return. Airlines had no method for getting rid of unsold
seats without impacting the prices of the other

seats. Walker's challenge was to come up with a way for airlines to boost revenues without affecting their fixed costs. He also had to factor in variables such as credit card companies, the Internet, marketing channels already in place, and electronic ticketing capabilities.

If I did this-and-such, what would go wrong? He asked the question many times as he refined his business model. Then he patented it and rolled out the site in 1998. During its first five years of operation, Priceline.com sold $4 billion worth of hotel reservations, airline tickets, car rentals and other services to over 10 million customers around the world.

"All success requires two disciplines— trying and learning from mistakes."

Born into slavery during the Civil War, George Washington Carver faced many struggles in his life. He did not attend school until age 11, and he had to support himself by doing odd jobs after classes. He was often shunned by fellow students because of his race.

He entered Iowa State University intending to study art, but a professor of agriculture saw that

Carver had a way with plants, experimenting to find different strains, and he convinced him to study agriculture instead. After receiving his master's degree, Carver was asked to start an agriculture program at the Tuskegee Institute in Alabama. To help poor blacks raise themselves out of poverty, Carver would teach them about the latest methods in farming, including replenishing soil that had been depleted by cotton and planting peanuts, sweet potatoes and soybeans. That would reduce their dependence on cotton and give them another cash crop as well as a means of sustenance.

Of all his challenges, this might have been Carver's toughest. His schoolroom was a shack, his students not very interested in tilling the soil. They had come to college to get away from that kind of life. To engage students during his lectures, he would draw them into conversations about nature and its secrets, and he would stress continually how important it was to help the less fortunate.

Carver's enthusiasm caught on. Four years after he started at Tuskegee, this country had a burgeoning peanut industry, and even a group of white planters took notice. They asked Carver to come and speak to them, and later requested that he go to Washington, DC to represent them in a Congressional debate over a tariff on peanuts from China.

In his lifetime, Carver developed over 280 food and consumer products made from peanuts, soybeans and sweet potatoes, including paints, face powders, toothpaste and building materials. Contrary to popular folklore, he did not invent peanut butter.

8. Invite Other Perspectives and Find Allies

Health care information technology is Todd Park and Jonathan Bush's business, though it didn't start out that way. In 1997 the two San Diego men had planned to buy a birthing clinic, learn how to run it, and then franchise the concept. They hadn't counted on the avalanche of paperwork, and they had no system for tracking outstanding insurance claims. Park's brother came up with a computer program to help them run the business, though they still could not make a go of it. They discovered, however, that using their system, they could offer claims processing services to other medical offices. That is how Athena Healthcare became Athena Health.

The company's web-based service helps doctors run the business part of their practices more efficiently—and more profitably, checking that patients have valid health insurance and verifying co-payment amounts before the first office visit. It then files claims on behalf of the provider, collects checks and makes the deposits. If a claim is rejected, it is examined to find out what went wrong.

At the center of the business is complex software that tries to incorporate every change in coding and billing address and every shift in regulations. A unique feature of the company is that it encourages employees to voice opinions and make suggestions for improvement. Customers are encouraged to do the same. Now that Athena Health has matured from its startup stage, Bush and Park have shifted the focus of the corporate culture from individualistic to collaborative.

"The best listeners are the best learners. The best learners qualify themselves to be the best leaders."

When Ronald Reagan was a boy, his mother always told him to look people straight in the eye, remember their names, and let them know that he cared. That was probably the reason that, during his years as president, he was known as the "Great Communicator."

Originally trained as an actor, Reagan became a public speaker when he was host of the TV program "General Electric Theater." GE hired him to tour the country and speak with people at all of its 139 plants. These conversations often turned to politics, a subject that began to interest Reagan more and more.

Years later he wrote, "Those GE tours became almost a postgraduate course in political science. I was seeing how government really operated and affected people in America, not how it was taught in school."

In 1966, Reagan ran for governor of California. In talking with people throughout the state, he used a technique he learned from his acting coaches—to imagine himself looking at the world through a character's eyes. He developed a knack for putting himself in someone else's shoes, and that helped him understand their thinking.

5

What Do You Expect?

"Success is like riding a bicycle. Either you keep moving or you fall down."

To achieve sustained success, expectations should never be vague or uncertain. These 7 principles are essential for two-way communication:

~ Understate and Overdeliver
~ Set Personal and Team Goals
~ Learn to Live with Criticism
~ Create Opportunities
~ Build on Past Performance
~ Plan Continuously
~ Focus on Results, Not Activities, Busyness or Babble

1. Understate and Overdeliver

"Moore's Law," describes an explosive trend in the design of computer hardware: the number of transistors that can be placed inexpensively on an integrated circuit increases exponentially, doubling approximately every two years. Processing speed, memory capacity and display resolution also improve at exponential rates. The law was named for Gordon Moore, one of the co-founders of Intel, who came up with the assessment in 1965.

> *"If you do not get what you want, it is a sign that you did not seriously want it."*
> —Rudyard Kipling, Author

Rebecca Halstead is barely five feet tall, but she has never let size get in her way. She applied to West Point when it opened its doors to women and won a spot in the class of 1981. Though she suffered some medical setbacks shortly after graduation, she overcame them by working even harder. She later persuaded her superior officer to give her a company command. Halstead served tours in the 101st Airborne and the 25th Infantry divisions, and she commanded the 10th Mountain Division Support Command when deployed to Afghanistan after 9/11. In 2005 she became the first female officer to be promoted to General Officer from the United States Military Academy when she was promoted to Brigadier General.

Strange Conclusions:

For those who watch what they eat, here's the final word on nutrition and health. It's a relief to know the truth after all those conflicting medical studies:

- ~ Japanese eat very little fat and suffer fewer heart attacks than Americans.
- ~ Mexicans eat a lot of fat and suffer fewer heart attacks than Americans.
- ~ Africans drink very little red wine and suffer fewer heart attacks than Americans.
- ~ The French drink excessive amounts of red wine and suffer fewer heart attacks than Americans.
- ~ Germans drink a lot of beer, eat lots of sausages and fatty food, but suffer fewer heart attacks than Americans.

Conclusion: Eat and drink what you like. Speaking English is apparently what kills you.

2. Set Personal and Team Goals

By nature, entrepreneurs and hands-on managers tend to be "control freaks" that have trouble delegating, largely because they are unwilling to trust others to do the job. Trust is all about risk, according to management professor Sally Atkinson, and the more fortune or reputation depend on someone else's performance, the more there is to lose.

How can you build a great team so that you feel comfortable letting go? By becoming a great boss. Management experts Sharon Jordan-Evans and Jeffrey Fox offer these suggestions:

~ Encourage total candor by asking for honest feedback.

~ Encourage loyalty by finding out what team members need from their jobs.

~ Be creative with rewards—surprise cash bonuses, gift certificates, time off.

~ Share information freely.

~ Set expectations of success, then check in periodically.

~ Don't be afraid to hire someone smarter or more talented than you are.

~ Observe team members in action. If you think there's room for improvement, schedule more training.

~ Devote 90% of your training time to high performers and potential high performers.

~ Give people the freedom to have fun.

"Individuals set personal goals. Teams must set team goals and succeed only when the team gets priority."

As a pitcher for the Brooklyn Dodgers, Sandy Koufax finished the 1961 season with an outstanding 18-13 record and 269 strikeouts. Only a year earlier, though, he was ready to quit the game because over his first six seasons with the team, his performance had been lackluster. A teammate advised him to ease up on his fastball so he could concentrate on throwing more accurately. That did the trick. By 1964 he had established himself as the best pitcher in baseball.

Though Koufax always aimed for a personal best, he went out of his way to be a team player. When Jeff Torborg came up from the minors, Koufax worked with the catcher to help him with pop-ups. Koufax refused to accept the award as best left-hander of the century unless Warren Spahn (a left-handed pitcher who played for 21 seasons, winning 20 games with a 23-7 record) was also honored. At a time when black players faced discrimination just trying to get a meal in a restaurant, Koufax would make it a point to greet them and sit with them. As a Jew, he knew about discrimination.

Workplace Personalities — Anyone You Know?

Employees, according to author Tim O'Leary, tend to fall into four distinct personality types. They are:

Warriors—use their natural aggressiveness and creativity, and fight the battles necessary to make their company successful.

Workers—are loyal and dependable, and they take direction well. They are the backbone of a business.

Whiners—spread discontent with their negativity and constant dissatisfaction.

Weasels—are lazy and unproductive.

Every company naturally needs to keep their warriors and workers and get rid of the weasels. It's the whiners who present the greatest challenge. While some of them are bent on infecting others with their dissatisfaction, O'Leary says that a whiner just might be "Sounding an alarm that you need to hear. When they're whining about a problem, I say, 'OK, let's look for a solution, and I'm going to put you in charge of that.' Oftentimes, you can transform them that way."

3. Learn to Live with Criticism

Few people have been more criticized than Jack Welch during his time as CEO of General Electric. The downsizing he was hired to engineer earned him the epithet "Hatchet Jack." There was the flap over his retirement package. There were the rumors about a messy affair and later divorce.

A great leader gets under the skin of every person in the company, he said, addressing a world business forum where he was given a hero's reception. When employees under perform, he added, a leader tells them so. And great leaders pick great successors.

> "The higher you go, the louder your critics become."

What to Do When an Opponent is Unreasonable:

~ Look for previous evidence of temper tantrums.

~ Prepare for the worst case.

~ Don't let bad behavior coerce you into doing the same.

~ Anticipate actions if talk becomes over-
heated.

~ Ask: "Is that what you really mean?"

~ Keep concentrating on your highest priorities.

~ Don't give up important points just to avoid
controversy.

~ Shift the discussion to less sensitive topics.

~ Ask for a brief recess to collect your
thoughts.

~ Walk away if progress is totally blocked.

> "Losers say 'If only I hadn't done this . . .
> Winners say, 'I think I'll try.'"

Comedian Bill Cosby feels strongly about the
need for African-Americans to learn and use
good English. He is severely criticized in many
places but continues to press his case. As he says:
"'Why you ain't.' 'Who you be.' 'What he
drive.' People marched and were hit in the face
with rocks to get an education, and now we've
got these knuckleheads walking around. We have
got to take the neighborhood back. Brown or
black versus the Board of Education is no longer
the white person's problem. We cannot blame the

white people any longer. We have to start holding each other to a higher standard."

"The best way to be remembered is to encourage those who want to improve."

4. Create Opportunities

Walt Disney was a creative genius who revolutionized the world of entertainment. He recognized early on that a constant flow of ideas was the lifeblood of the industry. He called it "plussing"—giving people a magical experience "plus" constantly improving on it—and he was wise enough to know he could not do it all himself.

To make a success of his enterprise, he had to emphasize the importance of "plussing" to his animators, engineers and staff, to convey his enthusiasm and then give them every opportunity to explore and experiment.

"Of all the things I have done," he once said, "the most vital is coordinating the talents of those who work for us and pointing them toward a certain goal."

> *"Opportunity does not appear,
> it is created."*

When Martin Edelston, founder of Bottom Line newsletter and other financial publications, complained to management guru Peter Drucker that his company meetings were boring, Drucker told him to try something different at the next meeting: ask everyone for suggestions on how to improve productivity.

Edelston did and was amazed at the result. Suggestions came faster than he could write them down, and at subsequent meetings the result was the same. Later he formalized the system and called it I-Power, and it has become central to the business. Employees are required to submit at least two ideas a week, usually by email. They rate the ideas themselves and the best ones are printed out in a monthly bulletin. The system uses cash awards from $5 to $100.

"Top-down management ignores the bedrock reality that everything a company needs to operate more efficiently is in the minds, hands and experience of its workers," Edelston says. "I have built my company on this simple premise."

Listening to employees and valuing their suggestions creates benefits apart from any the suggestions themselves might produce: it increases self-esteem and job satisfaction, which keeps turnover low.

> "Keep this in mind:
> Good things happening without work
> is luck. All luck is temporary."

Up until fairly recently in history, young girls were expected to become wives and mothers, and they received virtually no training for anything else. Juliette Gordon Low thought that should change. Low had a variety of interests—auto mechanics, gardening, flying, painting, even Morse code—and she believed that women could do anything if given the opportunity. On a trip to Scotland she met the founder of the British Boy Scouts and Girl Guides, Sir Robert Baden-Powell, and she envisioned creating a similar girls organization in America.

Shortly after her return to the U.S., Low called friends and said, "I've got something for the girls of Savannah, and all America, and all the world, and we're going to start it tonight." She told her friends to bring their daughters and their little sisters, neighbor girls and their friends.

That gathering on March 2, 1912 with 18 girls in attendance was the first American Girl Guide meeting. At subsequent weekly meetings, the girls were taught the basics of independent living and service to society, and they heard lectures about preparing for careers as professionals as well as learning the domestic arts.

Within two years, the Girl Scouts (as the group was now called) had over 1,000 members. As a result of their volunteer work during World War I, when they assisted the Red Cross and sold $9 million of Liberty Bonds, the Girl Scouts gained respect and recognition on a national level. By 1920, the organization had grown to 50,000. When Low died in 1927, there were 167,925 active members nationwide.

5. Build on Past Performance

"To better estimate future performance, examine results achieved in bad times."

How to Be Your Own Teacher

~ Reading will be your teacher—there is no limit to what you can learn from written words.

~ Responsibility will be your teacher—it will enable you to keep your promises.

~ Reputation will be your teacher—it will prevent compromising your principles.

~ Resilience will be your teacher—it will put you back on track.

~ Risk will be your teacher—it will prompt you to rise to new heights.

~ Reason will be your teacher—it will stop you from making serious mistakes.

~ Recovery will be your teacher—it will make you less dependent on others.

~ Reflection will be your teacher—it will cause you to look before you leap.

~ Rehearsal will be your teacher—it will reduce fear when it is time to perform.

~ Reliability will be your teacher—it will generate trust from those you need.

~ Restoration will be your teacher—it will reposition you for another try.

~ Resolve will be your teacher—it will prevent you from stopping too soon.

~ Readiness will be your teacher—it will give you confidence to face changes.

~ Resourcefulness will be your teacher—it will provide tools when you need them.

~ Renewal will be your teacher—it will prompt a positive outlook.

"A businessman who was near death asked that his remains be cremated and the ashes mailed to the Internal Revenue Service with the following note attached: 'Now you have it all.'"

Condoleezza Rice has faced many tough moments as President Bush's national security advisor and Secretary of State, especially with support for the Iraq war constantly eroding. More than one person has wondered how Rice, refined and soft-spoken, stands up to regular grilling by Congressional committees and the media.

Growing up black in segregated Birmingham, Alabama was a good start. Rice's parents and schoolteachers motivated her to take piano lessons starting at age three. Later, she took lessons in ballet, French, figure skating and tennis. At the University of Denver, on an honors scholarship, she ran into the notoriously racist professor William Shockley, who maintained that blacks were naturally inferior to whites and were holding back cultural evolution. In his class, Rice raised her hand and declared, "Let me tell you something. I speak French, I play Beethoven, I'm better at your culture than you are. Clearly, this can be taught."

She had intended to become a concert pianist but, convinced she wasn't good enough for that career, changed course and went into Soviet studies. At age 38 she became provost of Stanford University, the youngest person ever to occupy that position.

6. Plan Continuously

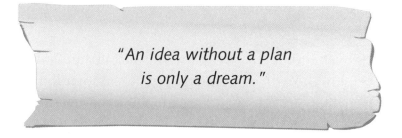

"An idea without a plan is only a dream."

"Temporal intelligence," the ability to simultaneously draw on the past, dream of the future, and tend to today, is a skill required for leadership and success. The good news is it can be learned. In *Time Mastery*, authors John Clemens and Scott Dalrymple maintain that each segment of time— what happened, what is happening, and what's going to happen—must get its proper attention.

People tend to live too much in the present, and that can make dreams and goals seem unreachable. To achieve temporal intelligence, try these exercises:

~ Write a paragraph about your company or department. Then circle all the verbs you used and categorize them into past, present or future tense. If you find many of the verbs falling into a single category, it may signal that you are getting stuck in your thinking.

~ Spring forward in time by creating a magazine dated some years in the future. Write articles about your company's new products/services/achievements. This will boost your ability to think in detail about where you're going.

Even though his company was facing a period of slow growth and intense price competition, General Electric CEO Jeffrey Immelt's enthusiasm about the future was evident in a speech he gave at Dartmouth College. His optimism derived from his willingness to set aside 20 percent of his time for thinking and develop new concepts. He believes coming up with "imagination breakthroughs" is key to success in his business. "Good leaders are very curious. They spend a lot of time trying to learn new things," he said. "A great part of this job is that I get to go places to pick up that next best idea."

> *"It is better to test your thoughts in writing than speaking. Criticism will be more accurate."*

7. Focus on Results, Not Activities, Busyness or Babble

As a grandchild of a former president of General Motors, Jessie O'Neill grew up in a servant-staffed mansion and had everything money could buy. She also knew the downside of inherited wealth—two cousins who committed suicide and her own alcoholism, depression and feelings of aimlessness. She documents her unhappiness in her 1996 book, *The Golden Ghetto*.

O'Neill got sober and then took 10 friends on a Caribbean cruise to celebrate her 40th birthday. The experience was so rewarding that she wanted to give more money away, and she has, donating much of her multimillion dollar inheritance to a variety of political and environmental causes. Then she launched The Affluenza Project, running workshops to help people like her avoid the pitfalls of having too much. No longer aimless, O'Neill says, "I feel as if I have done what I was put on earth to do."

*"Those who confuse activity
with results lose."*

Toyota Motor Corp believes its "five-why" analysis is the secret behind the company's successful products and record of quality. Whenever someone discovers a problem or defect, they put off looking for solutions until they ask the question "why?" enough times. Management believes that's the way to get to the root cause of a problem, which is the only way to fix it permanently.

"Five-why" concerns itself with taking the answer to the first "why?" and asking why it occurred, and then, why again. Usually, the root cause is uncovered after the fifth why. For example, an oil spill on the floor may be due to a leaking gasket. The oil could be cleaned up and the machine fixed, but that wouldn't necessarily eliminate the problem, which may be that a gasket is deteriorating, which may be the result of the manufacturer using inferior materials, which may be the result of something else.

The five-why approach has served Toyota well by eliminating production downtime and improving quality overall.

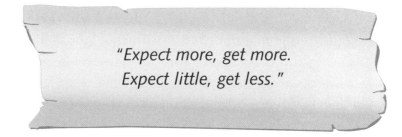

"Expect more, get more.
Expect little, get less. "

Why did the chicken cross the road?

Ralph Nader: The chicken's habitat on the other side of the road has been polluted by unchecked industrial greed. The chicken did not reach the unspoiled habitat on the other side of the road because it was crushed by the wheels of a gas –guzzling SUV.

Martha Stewart: No one called me to warn me which way that chicken was going. I had a standing order at the farmer's market to sell my eggs when the price dropped to a certain level. No little bird gave me any insider information.

Dr. Seuss: Did the chicken cross the road? Did he cross it with a toad? Yes, the chicken crossed the road, but why it crossed I've not been told.

Grandpa: In my day, we didn't ask why the chicken crossed the road. Somebody told us the chicken crossed the road, and that was good enough.

Bill Gates: I have just witnessed eChicken2007,

which will not only cross roads, but will lay eggs, file your important documents, and balance your checkbook. And . . . Internet Explorer is an integral part of Chicken.

Colonel Sanders: Did I miss one?

6

Losers Deny and Defer

> *"The most successful people are dejected by failure only briefly. Then they are surprised by it."*

Beware Ambitious Failures

Ambition is a valuable quality because it usually points to a self-starter. Unfortunately, it can also be almost completely self-centered. This type of "all eyes on me" person has a limited arena in which to be successful. Individual sports like golf, tennis and swimming come to mind. But when group effectiveness is needed, ambition must be controlled. If it is not:

~ Results are limited to what ambitious failures can do themselves.

~ Others become de-motivated to work because they know they will get no credit.

Ambitious failures:

~ Take precious time making sure everything focuses on them, especially microphones and video cameras.

~ Maneuver outcomes that favor their personal goals—not the team's.

~ Reward "devotees" and ignore key people working in the background.

~ Work hard to avoid situations where their weaknesses will become known.

~ Don't engage in conflict where their image may get tarnished, so we never know how strong they will be in tough times.

~ Seek projects where it is easy to shift blame for failure on others.

To benefit most from your own ambition, consider these clues:

~ A commitment without action is an empty glass.

~ A promise unkept is a debt unpaid.

~ Inspect what you expect before it is too late.

~ The shorter the learning time, the faster solutions can be found.

~ The faintest ink is better than the finest memory. Write it down!

~ Imagine your goal is a magnet. Have it pull you towards it.

You want to associate with self-starters, but how do you identify them? Look for people who:

~ Focus Energy and Avoid Distractions
~ Face Difficult Decisions
~ Add New Skills, Create New Choices and Avoid Dead Ends
~ Will Learn from Anyone, Anytime, Anywhere

1. Focus Energy and Avoid Distractions

"Inspiration does not incubate in evasion but in effort."

Leaders need to be creative, courageous, conscientious, and many other things, but the single most important quality of a leader, according to Marcus Buckingham, is the ability to rally others toward a better future. The author of *First, Break All the Rules*, the book that turned management theory on its ear, says that corporate America has greatly overcomplicated the leader's role. Because the future is an unknown quantity, people tend to fear it. The leader's role is to engage that fear and turn it into something positive, to distill a vision of the future and present it clearly so that people can see where they are headed.

"Leaders can't help but change the present, because the present isn't good enough," Buckingham says. "They succeed only when they find a way to make people excited by and confident in what comes next."

Trust is an issue that underlies every aspect of business, especially when teamwork is needed. When trust is breached for whatever reason, it must be rebuilt immediately. This involves much more than making a speech or sending a memo, say Dennis and Michelle Reina, co-authors of *Trust and Betrayal in the Workplace*. They recommend being pro-active by:

~ Letting team members know what the boundaries and expectations are through regular planning sessions and progress reviews, and daily 10-minute "stand-up" meetings.
~ Requiring team members to honor their agreements and be accountable for their actions.
~ Striving for the common good, with no hidden agendas.

~ Telling the truth, admitting mistakes and avoiding gossip.

"Effective leaders model the behavior they expect from others," the authors say.

> *"Most losers lose because they think they will."*

The year before Jackie Robinson broke the color barrier in baseball, Marion Motley was one of four black players to integrate professional football. The year was 1946. Motley had been working at an Ohio steel mill after leaving the military, and when the new All-American Football Conference was formed, he saw the chance to live out his dream of playing professional football. After joining the Cleveland Browns, he kept that dream in focus despite the racism he and fellow black player Bill Willis faced. They were not allowed to play in Florida, which had segregation laws, and Motley received a death threat before a game in Texas. Opposing players taunted them continually with racist remarks.

To keep the door open for other black players, though, he had to avoid retaliation on the field.

"If either Willis or I had been hotheads and gotten into fights and things like that, it would have put things back 10 years," Motley said. In his career, he played offense and defense on five title teams and in 1968 was the second black player inducted into the Pro Football Hall of Fame.

2. Face Difficult Decisions

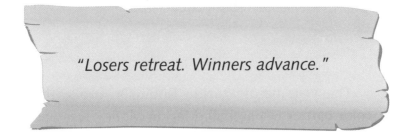

"Losers retreat. Winners advance."

Darwin Award Winners

First place: When his 38-caliber revolver failed to fire at his intended victim during a holdup in Long Beach, California, would-be robber James Elliot did something that can only inspire wonder. He peered down the barrel and tried the trigger again. This time, it worked.

And now, the honorable mentions:

~ After stopping for drinks at an illegal bar, a Zimbabwean bus driver found that the 20 mental patients he was supposed to be transporting from Harare to Bulawayo had escaped. Not wanting to admit his incompetence, the driver went to a nearby bus stop and offered everyone waiting there a free ride. He then delivered the passengers to the mental hospital, telling the staff that the patients were very excitable and prone to bizarre fantasies. The deception wasn't discovered for three days.

~ A man walked into a Louisiana Circle-K, put a $20 bill on the counter, and asked for change. When the clerk opened the cash drawer, the man pulled a gun and demanded all the cash in the register, which the clerk promptly provided. The man took the cash from the clerk and fled, leaving the $20 bill on the counter. The total amount of cash he got from the drawer: $15. (If someone points a gun at you and gives you money, is a crime committed?)

~ As a female shopper exited a New York convenience store, a man grabbed her purse and ran. The clerk called 911 immediately, and the woman was able to give them a detailed description of the thief. Within minutes the police apprehended him, put him in the car and drove back to the store. The thief was then taken out of the car and told to stand there for a positive ID. To which he replied, "Yes, officer, that's her. That's the lady I stole the purse from."

~ The Ann Arbor News crime column reported that a man walked into a Burger King in

Ypsilanti, Michigan at 4 A.M., flashed a gun and demanded cash. The clerk turned him down. He said he couldn't open the cash register without a food order. When the man ordered onion rings, the clerk said they weren't available for breakfast. The man, frustrated, walked away.

And the 5-Star Stupidity Award Winner: When a man attempted to siphon gasoline from a motor home parked on a Seattle street, he got much more than he bargained for. Police arrived at the scene to find a very sick man curled up next to a motor home near spilled sewage. A police spokesman said that the man admitted to trying to steal gasoline and plugged his siphon hose into the motor home's sewage tank by mistake. The owner of the vehicle declined to press charges, saying that it was the best laugh he'd ever had.

> *"The way to develop self-confidence is to do the thing you fear and get a record of successful experiences behind you."*
> —William Jennings Bryan, lawyer, politician

The best example yet of a terribly belated and woefully half-hearted apology was in Pete Rose's book, *My Prison without Bars*. He admitted that his gambling habit made him bet on the team he managed, the Cincinnati Reds, an unacceptable breach of conduct. But he also wrote, "I'm sure that I'm supposed to act all sorry or sad or guilty now that I've accepted that I've done something wrong. But you see I'm just not built that way."

If Rose were a person of greater integrity with a true sense of accountability, he might have followed the example of Hall of Famer Mickey Mantle. Diagnosed with alcohol-related liver disease, Mantle made the decision to speak publicly and honestly about the destructive nature of his lifestyle. He cautioned young people not to look to him as a role model, and he went on to become a spokesman for organ donations.

"A lie cuts both ways. The hearer is deceived and the teller is never trusted again."

The 5 Key Components of Trust

Trust builds relationships, and building relationships is fundamental to success. In *The 12 Clichés of Selling*, author Barry Farber offers these essential ingredients for establishing trust:

- ~ Truth, because lying is the number one way to lose business.
- ~ Reliability, because people need to know they can count on you.
- ~ Understanding, because you are attempting to see the world through the other person's eyes.
- ~ Service, because when you go above and beyond, you create added value.
- ~ Patience, because it's the little things you do over time that make the difference.

3. Add New Skills, Create New Choices and Avoid Dead Ends

> *"Procrastination is not accidental. It is deliberate and has the same effect as paralysis."*

Story Musgrave's life had a rocky beginning. Both of his parents were alcoholics who committed suicide, as did a brother. As a boy, Musgrave would find solace from the daily domestic chaos in the fields of his family's Massachusetts dairy farm, lying in the grass under the blue sky, with the mountains and forests surrounding him. He read the nature writings of Emerson, Whitman and Thoreau and gained an understanding of the importance of self-reliance.

After a stint in the Marines, which he joined to get experience away from home, he realized he wanted more study, and enrolled in Syracuse University. That was the beginning of a love affair with learning, and over the years he earned degrees in mathematics, chemistry, biophysics, psychology and literature. Along the way, he also became a medical doctor.

Musgrave entered NASA's astronaut program and flew six space missions in a 30-year career. While in space, he wrote hundreds of poems about the experience. When he wasn't orbiting the earth, he worked part-time as a surgeon at Denver General Hospital and part-time as a professor of biophysics and physiology at the University of Kentucky Medical Center. As if that were not enough to keep him busy, he also trained as a pilot and parachutist.

One his Musgrave's most notable achievements was his repair of the Hubble telescope in outer space. Though pleased with the success of the mission, he said, "I was incredibly happy that it worked, but you just have to keep going in victory as I would have in defeat." He puts a positive spin on the mistakes he makes. "I fail all the time," he says, "but I learn from that."

> *"Indifference is a handicap, but laziness is a sin."*

How to Negotiate Successfully

When both sides are determined to make a deal, they usually do. To make this possible they:

~ Provide the background needed to clarify their position.

~ Ask questions until the other position is absolutely understood.

~ Give and get objective evidence and facts, not opinions.

~ Don't reject opposing ideas too soon.

~ Agree and disagree honestly, avoiding mind games.

~ Disarm by agreeing whenever they can.

~ Avoid inflammatory words to retain the relationship.

~ Reject ideas without rejecting the deliverer.

"Winners are wonderers who
decide. Losers are wanderers who
continue to wander."

4. Will Learn from Anyone, Anytime, Anywhere

"A mediocre idea that generates
enthusiasm will go further than a great
idea that inspires no one."

—Mary Kay Ash, Cosmetics Executive

Roger Maris became famous as the baseball
player who broke Babe Ruth's single season
home-run record during the Yankee's 1961 season. He twice won the American League's Most
Valuable Player award.

Yet his entry into the sport wasn't at all spectacular. The Chicago Cubs called him up from the
minors, but were unimpressed after watching
him hit and field. The Cleveland Indians made

him an offer to play in their minor league division, which he accepted. During his first season in 1953, he batted .325 in 418 at bats, with 9 home runs and 80 runs batted in.

Maris worked continually to improve his statistics, even in the off-season. He was always asking coaches for batting tips that would help him improve his swing. Each year, he moved up in the ranks until he reached the majors four years later as the Indians' right fielder. The following year he was traded to the Kansas City Athletics, and in 1960 joined the New York Yankees. They played in the World Series that year and for the next three years.

Throughout his career, Maris stayed focused on his game, putting all his effort into every play. He sprinted for fly balls, swung his bat hard and straight, dived into bases. When he broke his hand during the 1965 season, the Yankees traded him to the St. Louis Cardinals. In 1967 and again in 1968, Maris led that team to the World Series.

"Problems are only opportunities in work clothes."

—Henry J. Kaiser, Industrialist

When George Mercherle traveled the back roads of Illinois selling insurance to farmers, he heard nothing but complaints about the high cost of premiums. At the time, everyone was charged the same rate. But farmers wondered why they, who drive the back roads, should pay the same as city drivers, who are more likely to have an accident. Mercherle took their complaints to his bosses, who told him that if he didn't like the way they were doing business, he should start his own company.

He did—Mecherle is the founder of State Farm Insurance—which started a revolution in the industry. He was a farmer himself who read constantly to learn how to improve crop yields and take care of livestock and machinery. Now that he was embarking on a new enterprise, he used the same approach. He studied everything he could find about the insurance industry, how it was structured, and where it could be improved.

He decided on a mutual insurance association, which would be owned by its policyholders, and set up rates based on how likely a person was to have a car accident. He promoted this radical concept at farm associations around Illinois and soon had enough capital to launch his company on June 7, 1922. He had no trouble signing up clients, who were attracted by rates that were 30% less than most other insurers.

Today, State Farm is the largest property and casualty insurance company in the country.

> *"Successful people change when they should . . . and before they must."*

7

The Sources of Confidence

We prosper in life not because of what happens to us but because of what we make happen. We move forward as we gain confidence and make necessary adjustments to both failure and success.

The greatest single advantage for any person, beyond good physical and mental health, comes from parents who are exemplary role models. Next would be their opportunities to learn from effective leaders whose legacy transmitted confidence and competence to be successful in their career. They strengthen them to *carry on* because:

- We are stronger as a result of their influence
- We are more alert to opportunities
- We have learned to support each other
- We have learned to endure hardship
- We are more aware of our strengths and how to use them

- We do not quit when discouraged
- We resist being manipulated
- We motivate ourselves without prompting
- We know when and how to get needed help
- We are more confident in ourselves

The legacy real leaders leave is . . . *carry on!*

Confidence increases when we:

~ Rebound from Failure
~ Find the Help Needed
~ Build On and Benefit From Strengths
~ Persevere
~ Become Self-Motivated
~ Take Calculated Risks
~ Meet Commitments
~ Learn from Experience

1. Rebound from Failure

"Unconfessed guilt never finds peace."

You can't fail if you don't take risks . . . but you also can't succeed. The trick is to embrace your mistakes and learn from them, says Dr. Charles

Manz, a professor of leadership at the University of Massachusetts. Here's what he suggests:

~ Remove the pain. Once you're past the gloom, sit back and analyze the facts as if you were a scientist. Tell yourself the failure was simply an experiment that had a different result from the one you expected.

~ Search for reasons. Was it bad timing, a flaw in your logic, an incorrect assumption? If you can figure out what went wrong, you can avoid making the mistake again.

~ View failure as a step in the process. Once we know what doesn't work, new ideas can spring to mind.

~ Don't go half way. If you have put your heart and soul into your efforts, you can at least eliminate that as the cause of your failure.

~ Stay cool. Failure is an opportunity to test yourself. If you can avoid falling apart, that alone will give you the courage to try again.

"Self-confident people sometimes fail . . . but not for long."

When Henry J. Heinz's first food processing company went bankrupt, he carried around a notebook with the names of each of his creditors and the letters "MO"—Moral Obligations—written on the cover. Though this was the worst time of his life, though he experienced depression and self-doubt, he was determined to pay back every cent he owed. With help from his family, he did, and in less than a year's time.

Now Heinz brought his brother and his cousin into the business and renamed the company F&J Heinz. Instead of a single product—prepared horseradish—he manufactured many prepared foods. Heinz "57 Varieties" was heavily advertised to the growing number of busy housewives who, he believed, would welcome what he called "a pure article of superior quality." He had no hesitation in offering a money-back guarantee.

Later in his life, when a group of financiers tendered an offer to buy his company, Heinz turned them down. "We are working for success and not for money," he told them. "The money part will take care of itself."

"Unless we have overcome failure, success has no joy."

The Pursuit of Happyness is the modern day rags-to-riches tale of Chris Gardner, who found himself homeless and destitute when a new job failed to materialize and his girlfriend locked up their house and left town with all his belongings and their son. A sympathetic manager at a brokerage firm gave him a job as a trainee and a monthly stipend of $1,000. Gardner set a goal of making 200 cold calls a day, and he studied for the stockbroker exam on his own time.

In pricey San Francisco, his stipend didn't go far. He sometimes slept at the office. He wore one suit and carried the other, along with his books and toiletries, so he could stay mobile. "Whenever worries about what I couldn't control overcame me, my focus saved me," Gardner wrote. "When my brain wanted to give up, my attitude was that I had to study like I was in prison—because knowledge was power and freedom."

He passed his exam with a score well above what he needed to get a license, and in no time he went from trainee to full-fledged broker. Just as he was getting on his feet, the girlfriend showed up, handed him his son, and left again.

Now Gardner had another set of problems, including where to stay with a child (his rooming house wouldn't allow them). With the help of a minister who ran the neighborhood soup kitchen and shelter, Gardner was eventually able to rent an apartment and put his son in day care. A few

years later, Bear Stearns recruited him for its San
Francisco office. By 1987, he had done well
enough to open his own brokerage firm, Gardner
Rich & Co., in Chicago.

"I learned that not succeeding is OK," Gardner
said, "but giving up isn't."

2. Find the Help Needed

A former football player and founder of the commercial real estate empire that bears his name,
Roger Staubach has always followed the wisdom
of Abraham Lincoln, i.e., to surround himself
with people who are smarter than he is. In his
athletic career he won a Heisman Trophy, quarter-
backed the Dallas Cowboys to two Super Bowl
wins, and was named Most Valuable Player in
Super Bowl VI. In 1977, after learning the real estate business in the off-seasons, he founded his
company.

Staubach has applied the lessons he learned on
the football field to the business world. "What
makes you successful," he says, "are the people in
the huddle."

"Success is achieved in 2 ways:
Hiring hard workers
Avoiding loafers"

At a time in our country's history when mills and sweatshops made the average worker's life pure drudgery, Harvey Firestone was offering his employees health benefits, free life insurance, and eight-hour work days—in addition to higher than average wages. If they wished, they could participate in easy payment plans to purchase company-built homes and company stock.

"The successful businessman . . . gives as much thought, or more, to the welfare of his employees as he does to the profits of the business," he once said. Firestone believed that by motivating employees in this way, they would help him manufacture the best tires. At the time of his death in 1938, Firestone Tire & Rubber Co. was producing 25 percent of the automobile and truck tires on American roadways.

"To better influence improvements in someone else, first consider how you might change yourself."

3. Build On and Benefit From Strengths

Because of his clear sightedness, Ronald Reagan left a rich legacy for both his country and the world. A president with a deep sense of commitment and the ability to focus intensely, he believed passionately in his vision—he called it "Morning in America"—and shaped public opinion around it. That focus inspired loyalty in those close to him, because, as a former aide said, "He brought out the best in others."

He also influenced world leaders. His alliance with Prime Minister Margaret Thatcher helped recast the political landscape in England. He showed Mikhail Gorbachev what people in a free society can work to achieve when he took the Soviet leader on a helicopter ride over one of Reagan's favorite neighborhoods. Today, there is no more Soviet Union. Russia is a free nation.

> *"People who don't feel good about themselves also complicate the lives of those nearby."*

The Ball brothers, Frank and Edmund, watched their Buffalo, NY, factory burn to the ground one winter night in 1886. The plant manufactured tin and glass containers. Only the year before, when the patent for the Mason Improved Fruit Jar expired, the brothers had jumped on the opportunity to begin making their own glass fruit jars. They had a new seven-pot coal-burning glass furnace and big plans for the future. That first year, they produced 12,500 of the popular fruit jars.

Then came the fire. What could have been the end, however, was only the beginning for the Ball brothers. Their plant was insured, but instead of rebuilding in New York, the brothers decided to move their operation to Muncie, Indiana, where a nearby natural gas well would provide cheap power. And they continued to look for opportunities. When the patent on the Mason porcelain-lined cap expired, they added that to their line.

The Ball brothers made a good team. While Edmund turned his attention to the factory, figuring out better and better methods of production, Frank scanned the horizon for new opportunities. In 1893, they bought the patent for a process that allowed them to do away with the blowpipe method of glassmaking. It didn't work on an assembly line, so the brothers developed their own machine that eliminated the need to grind the jars to make them smooth. Over the years, though they continued to improve manufacturing processes to increase production and cut costs, it was never at the expense of quality.

By 1998, Ball Corp. had $2.9 billion in revenue.

*"Opportunity may be accidental,
learning is not."*

4. Persevere

You might say that Wayne Huizenga has the ability to turn garbage into gold. The founder of AutoNation and the chain of video stores known as Blockbuster launched his career in the late 1950s as the manager of a trash collection service, a job offered to him by a family friend. A few months later, he saw a newspaper ad for a truck route that promised revenues of $500 a month. Huizenga jumped at the opportunity. Though he had no money to buy the route outright, the owner agreed to finance the deal. A few years later, Huizenga incorporated his first business, Southern Sanitation Service. He would take that company public in 1971, turn it into Waste Management, and eventually land a spot on the Fortune 1000 list.

He could have retired then, but in the mid-1980s a friend steered him toward another investment idea and Huizenga could not resist taking a look. This time it was a video store. Huizenga did not even own a VCR, but he could see the potential in the enterprise the minute he walked in the door. "This is something completely different," he recalls saying. "It's a heck of a business." He and his friend bought into the company, took it national, and over the next half dozen years averaged a store opening every 17 hours.

Meanwhile, Huizenga was turning his attention to sports, and for a while he owned the Miami Dolphins football team, the Florida Marlins baseball team, and the Florida Panthers hockey team. He is still the majority owner of the Dolphins.

Huizenga can't help but keep on keeping on. He regularly lectures at the H. Wayne Huizenga School of Business & Entrepreneurship at Nova Southeastern University in Florida. "If you're going to be an entrepreneur," he says, "it's not all textbooks . . . It's a feeling you have that you can do this and make it happen."

> *"The most successful people are the hardest to torment."*

Major-league pitchers have a job that's wearing on the body, so Nolan Ryan's record 27-year career is something of a miracle. In fact, Ryan's autobiography is titled "Miracle Man." In it he says, "You're not going to get very far until you have a burning desire to excel."

In 1972, struggling with a mediocre record, he had been traded from the New York Mets to the California Angels. At the Angels' facility, he discovered a weight room and got to work. At the time, weight training for baseball players was discouraged because it was thought to rob them of flexibility, but Ryan believed he needed that training to become better conditioned and develop the necessary stamina. "Once you fatigue, it affects your mechanics," he said. "You can no longer pitch with the precise timing required for a smooth, compact motion."

At age 44—ancient by baseball standards—Ryan was able to pitch his seventh no-hitter, and he had no doubt that without the weight training, he would have been out of the game years before.

"For those unsure of themselves, most relationships are short and shallow."

5. Become Self-Motivated

*"When cheers are your only motivation,
your self confidence is zero."*

Clif Bars pioneered the market for a power-packed source of nutrition. With $1,000 in savings, founder Gary Erickson began selling the energy bars in 700 bike stores on the West Coast in 1992. He introduced an energy drink five years later, and came out with Luna bars for women in 1999. Luna bars added $10 million in sales its first year.

After a spectacular climb, Erickson saw sales slip, after food giants Kraft and Nestle got into the game with PowerBar and Balance Bar. Those companies had marketing resources Erickson couldn't even begin to match, yet when another food giant offered him $120 million for his company, he turned them down. The buyout would have meant moving the company from the Bay area to the Midwest and saying goodbye to his 65 employees. Even more important, Erickson did not want to lose the qualities in his corporate culture that he had worked to establish, including backing a number of social causes.

"I would rather poke needles in my eyes than have someone calling me every day saying, 'I need this report' or 'I need to know how your numbers are,'" he says of his rationale for staying independent. "It would drive me nuts."

Clif has been holding its own. Erickson eschews big bucks advertising in favor of grassroots marketing to athletes, internet campaigns, and public relations efforts centered around carefully chosen venues. It's a constant struggle, but being independent of corporate overseers allows Erickson the freedom to pursue his vision.

> *"If you aren't fired with enthusiasm, you will be fired with enthusiasm."*
> —Vince Lombardi, football coach

When Lynette Hayden went from welfare to work as a cleaner for Catholic Charities of Chicago, she got more than a job and a paycheck. She got motivated to keep on working. Even though her son, Kelvin, plays for the Indianapolis Colts, earns a minimum of six figures a year, and could easily support her, Lynette claims that having a regular job offers her not only a sense of purpose, but also friendships with co-workers. To the question, "Why don't you stop working now?" she responds with a question of her own: "Why would I quit just because my son plays in the NFL?"

6. Take Calculated Risks

CEOs need to be in control, yet they know that new ideas can't emerge unless employees are empowered to propose them. Steven Khail, the director of investor relations for heavy equipment manufacturer Manitowoc, wanted to put together the Wisconsin company's first "analyst day." CEO Terry Growcock had to give it some thought. He had always believed in an open door policy: Not only did he believe in sharing information to help people understand management's vision, every employee in the company had the right to ask questions and to challenge him. He also believed that when you authorized someone to get a job done, you could not second-guess that person along the way.

So he took a deep breath and then gave Khail the green light. Khail kept Growcock in the loop on the logistics of the event as well as the format and content of the presentation. "In the end, this was Steve's project," Growcock said. "It wasn't necessarily how I would have done [everything], but he was empowered and it was very successful."

"To expect change in others but not yourself is the hope of a fool."

During his second tour of duty in Iraq, Marine corporal Robert Mitchell was part of "Operation Phantom Fury," a ground invasion force charged with taking back Fallujah. It was rumored that the city was being used to train foreign terrorists, and Marines were their targets. The fighting was fiercer than any they had ever experienced. The marines were waging the battle house by house. As they broke down the door of one house, they were met with a barrage of grenade and rifle fire.

Taking cover in a bathroom with two wounded fellow Marines—Mitchell was also wounded—he applied tourniquets to stem the bleeding and then ran back into the living room to help evacuate the other casualties, killing one of their enemies with his knife. When all the Marines were outside, they leveled the house with C4 explosives, killing the remaining terrorists.

In presenting Mitchell with the Navy Cross, one of the highest honors awarded for battlefield heroism, Marine Lt. Gen. John Sattler said, "He did not go forward in a crazed moment or on an impulse. He thought things through and he did what needed to be done."

"You cannot lead for long without having your own emotions under control."

7. Meet Commitments

"Winning can be good. Achieving self-imposed goals is better."

As a young businessman, David Packard took issue with an expert who claimed that management's sole responsibility is to its shareholders. Packard believed that it also has a responsibility to employees, customers, and the community at large. Though he was practically laughed out of the room, he never changed his opinion.

In fact, the man who founded Hewlett-Packard formulated that belief into a management philosophy known as the HP Way, and it helped build the company to $20 billion in annual sales. Its premise was simple: When workers, customers and managers are happy, everyone profits.

A prime component of the HP Way is placing trust in employees, especially those who come into contact directly with customers. A sense of humor is also important. Packard met frequently with employees, even as the company grew. One employee, working at H-P's King of Prussia facility outside of Philadelphia, extended his hand and introduced himself. "Joe Jones, King of Prussia," he said.

Packard's response: "Dave Packard, no title."

"The shortest route to rapid success in any field is to deliver more than expected."

Number one on Olympic skier Nancy Morgan's list of traits that all champions have in common is "commitment to the fundamentals." That means mastering new skills and techniques, and developing new strengths. Not getting it right the first time shouldn't be a reason to give up, she says. Other traits of champions are:

~ Enthusiasm—You need burning, white hot desire or you will never be better than average.

~ Alliances—All champions surround themselves with a strong support team.

~ Self-confidence—Believe in yourself.

~ Focus—Life is a series of tests; we must pass each one to move on.

"Do something every day that scares you out of your comfort zone," Morgan adds. "Feeling a little awkward is a natural outcome of gaining new strengths."

> "When it's the right thing. . . .
> just do it!"

8. Learn from Experience

> "Uncertain leaders cause dissention, diversion and ultimately disaster."

What Good Is Experience?

Experience is the best teacher, you say. But is it? Sometimes yes, sometimes no. It all depends on you. Too often, what we call experience is nothing but repetition. If experience is to be valuable, we must not only *learn* from it, we must *apply* it and improve.

Experience can be good if:

- It has prepared you for today.
- You are comfortable with change.
- You welcome new ideas.
- You scan the horizon for competitive advantage.
- You never stop exploring.
- You change wrongs before they become habits.
- You learn to simplify, not complicate.
- You can apply it to current problems.
- You are committed to renewal.
- You use it to stretch to new heights.

Experience can be bad if:

- Your skills are out of date.
- You are locked into past habits.
- You resist change.
- You keep reliving "the good old days."
- You fear making mistakes.
- You apply old solutions to new problems.
- You waste energy on regrets.
- You seek comfort in repetition.
- You dwell too long on past accomplishments.
- You have followed the wrong people.

"Life Lesson #1:
It takes many years to become
an overnight success. "

8

Avoiding the Comfort Zone (Get Back in Line)

Let's be realistic. When we have a tough job to do, we don't ask someone whose main objectives have been safety and comfort. We look for a track record of accomplishment in dealing with serious problems and difficult situations. These signal flags are trustworthy:

~ How Competence is Converted into Actual Accomplishment
~ What is the Evidence of Goal Achievement

~ Handling Multiple Priorities
~ Effective Use of Time and Resources
~ Initiative
~ Teamwork
~ Coping with Conflict and Adversity

1. How Competence is Converted into Actual Accomplishment

Everyone has a theory about how to manage effectively. Some people have grown rich offering the latest, hottest idea. George Hansen, the CEO of Corporate Lodging Consultants, admits, "I've fallen victim to the latest management theory as many times as the next guy." Yet when the Red Cross asked him to help relocate thousands of people who had been displaced by Hurricane Katrina, Hansen realized that none of those management theories were going to be of any use to him.

At first, he turned the Red Cross down. He didn't think his company had the resources. Then, as the dimensions of the disaster became apparent, he rallied his 125 employees and over the Labor Day weekend they faxed every hotel in their system. In 48 hours, they had found discounted hotel space for 250,000 storm victims.

Hanson says that it was a wonderful lesson in how people who know they are doing something important will put their heads together to find solutions. "There is no perfect structure. You have to find what fits you."

There was a time not long ago when the only reason a female would be in the executive suite was if she was serving the coffee. It's a measure of how far we've come as a society that women have now joined the ranks of CEOs of Fortune 500 companies. Financially speaking, 2006 was a very good year for these companies headed by women:

Rite Aid—Mary Sammons
Reynolds American—Susan Ivey
Avon Products—Andrea Jung
Xerox—Anne Mulcahy
Safeco—Paula Rosput Reynolds
PepsiCo—Indra Nooyi
Sara Lee—Brenda Barnes
ADM—Patricia Woertz
EBay—Meg Whitman

"Big jobs usually go to those who prove their ability to outgrow small ones."
—Ralph Waldo Emerson, poet

In the years he spent as CEO of General Electric, Jack Welch showed the world how one of America's oldest and largest companies could still act nimbly and embrace the future. GE was one of the first companies to build the Internet into its daily operations. It restructured its business units and made a play for a more global presence. When Welch took over in 1981, GE's market value was $13 billion. By 2000, its value had risen to more than $500 billion. Moreover, Welch had groomed so many outstanding managers that other companies competed to hire them. Asked for his advice to anyone looking to start their own company, he said, "Surround yourself with people better than you. That's absolutely critical."

"No interesting work is ever hard."
—Henry Ford, Industrialist

We may grumble about the health care system in this country, yet in some parts of the world, there is no system at all. As a fourth year medical student volunteering at a hospital in Tanzania, Edward O'Neil was shocked to see patients suffering with polio, malaria, leprosy and tuberculosis—diseases that had been virtually eradicated in the West. For most of the patients, the treatment he rendered was the first they had ever received. Dr. O'Neil was determined to remedy that situation.

In 1998, after writing two books on health, poverty and global service, he founded Omni Med, a non-profit organization that recruits doctors to train medical personnel in third world countries and establish continuing medical education programs. The first program was launched in Belize, and since has branched into Guyana, Kenya and Thailand. O'Neil serves as the organization's president, without pay, and donates an additional 30 hours a week and a portion of his annual income to the group.

"Some friends think I am crazy to do this," O'Neil said. "This is the intersection of ethics and ability, and this, to me, is exactly what I should be doing." Next he would like to create a global health corps, a plan that is undergoing discussion in the Senate.

2. What is the Evidence of Goal Achievement

There were not many opportunities for a black man to make money in the 1930s. Archie Moore took the one most open to him—boxing—and began fighting professionally at age 23. Because that is old for a boxer, he had to train long and hard. He'd walk stairs on his hands and practice throwing punches, using his aunt's five-pound flatirons as weights. "I had the best jab in the business," Moore once said, "Joe Louis notwithstanding."

In the ring, Moore had a style all his own, always waiting for his opponent to throw the first punch, meanwhile bobbing and weaving continuously. He earned the nickname "The Mongoose" because of his bait-and-dodge technique.

As his reputation grew and he became a contender for the middleweight crown, he found it increasingly difficult to arrange matches. Highly ranked boxers didn't want to risk losing to this fearsome newcomer. In his campaign to pursue a title shot, Moore wandered from town to town, trying to arrange fights. He wrote dozens of letters to sports writers asking them to back him. Always, he remembered what his first manager, Cal Thompson, told him: "You've got to look, think and act like a champion."

It took Moore 16 years to win his title as world light heavyweight champion. He was 39. He continued to fight for another decade, retiring in 1963 with a record of 194 wins out of 228 bouts.

"Credibility is based on promises compared to results."

Historians consider the architect Daniel Burnham to be the inventor of modern city planning, with his innovative designs and bold use of the latest technologies. He is famous for this legendary utterance: "Make no little plans. They have no magic to stir men's blood."

But as a young man, Burnham traveled a rocky road. He took the entrance exams for Harvard and Yale, and failed them both, even though his father had paid for prep school and tutors. He ran for the state senate and was defeated. For a brief time, he tried mining silver out West. He returned to Chicago, met the architect John Root, and the two opened their own firm. Their hopes were high, but the famous Panic of 1873 spun the economy into a depression. Some clients, out of money, offered clothing as barter for services; Burnham had to take a part-time job outside the firm to keep it afloat.

What Burnham did have in abundance, though, was an ability to focus intensely and a willingness to be patient. The invention of the passenger elevator and the steel frame allowed him to envision the construction of buildings that were taller than ever before. The Montauk Building was the world's first "skyscraper;" it was 10 stories high. Burnham was the consulting architect for the 1893 World's Columbian Exhibition. Years later he led the redesign of Cleveland and the planning for an expanded City of Chicago.

"The gap between strength and weakness is called persistence."

Craig Breedlove raced his first car at age 16—a 1934 Ford Hot Rod Coupe—and has been hooked on the thrill ever since. He wanted to be like the drivers he watched attempting to break speed records at the Bonneville Salt Flats. When he learned that for $500 he could buy a surplus jet engine, he started working two jobs to raise the money, even though he was still in school.

He came up with a model of the car he wanted to race, the Spirit of America, which was sitting half-built in his back yard. "I had to make progress on my own before I could interest a sponsor," he said. After finagling his way into the office of the district manager at Shell Oil Company, Breedlove presented his case for sponsorship. The meeting, which lasted several hours, ended with the district manager agreeing to help. There was a series of meetings with other Shell executives, who turned them down. Breedlove was undiscouraged. "I wouldn't take no for an answer," he said. Finally the head of Shell's U.S. marketing agreed to sponsor the project; later, Goodyear also came on board.

On August 6, 1963, Breedlove set his first land speed record—407 m.p.h. He went on to break the 500 m.p.h. and then the 600 m.p.h. speed records. His attempts to set a 700 m.p.h. record both failed, but that hasn't ended Breedlove's quest. "Quitting," he says, "is the only way you'll ensure that you won't succeed."

3. Handling Multiple Priorities

The Good Boss Checklist

An analysis of information obtained from more than 5,000 employees working for more than a dozen business and government agencies identifies ten qualities needed by leaders, regardless of age, sex, industry or size, location, organizational structure or corporate culture of the company. They must:

- Provide clear direction
- Encourage open, two-way communication
- Be willing to coach and support people
- Provide "objective" recognition
- Establish ongoing controls
- Select accountable people
- Understand the financial implications of decisions
- Encourage innovation and new ideas
- Make clear-cut decisions

• Consistently demonstrate high levels of integrity

Rate yourself on each item from 1 (Poor) to 5 (Excellent). Then compare the results. Set specific goals in each of the areas where improvement is needed most.

> *"Job Thermometer: Unless you are solving problems, your work isn't important and you're probably not accomplishing much."*

NBA commissioner David Stern has what he calls "a complex set of businesses" to operate in. He has to deal not only with the players, but also with television stations, sponsors and fans. When he began his tenure in 1984, playoff games used to be broadcast in tape-delay and relegated to late-night TV. Stern knew that to make the NBA more attractive to its various markets, he would have to change its image. One of the first things he did was implement a tough anti-drug program—a first for professional sports—and take a hard line on violence, using fines and suspensions to keep players in line. Then he made players more accessible to the media, showcasing them as among the best athletes on the planet.

"What has worked for me is demonstrating to the people who you're expecting to follow you that you believe in what you're doing and what they're doing . . . and you're willing to do it along with them, if that's what's necessary to get the job done."

Using plenty of marketing savvy and a employing a global vision, Stern helped boost NBA revenues tenfold and expand viewership to 121 countries.

> *"When you think you have the answer, don't brag about it—use it!"*

How can you set yourself up for a promotion at work, even when others are being downsized? By being your own "kingmaker." That's the advice of TV executive and entrepreneur Joanne Cini. Here are a few of her tips:

~ Master each position you're given to gain broad experience as you move up the ladder.
~ Be a strong performer, a multi-tasker, and prove yourself in a variety of roles.

~ Neutralize critics by being gracious when you make a mistake.

~ Take action if you see something wrong. It's a good way to learn about the integrity of your company.

~ Make these efforts every day. "The way you handle yourself on a daily basis speaks volumes compared with an hour-long interview when the job you want is open," Cini says.

4. Effective Use of Time and Resources

"There are times when those who conform are as dangerous as cowards."

Bob Feller had an amazing talent on the baseball field and his father, Bill, was wise enough to know how to help him develop it. Though the family's Iowa farm required long hours of labor, Bill found time to play catch regularly with his son. As Bob's arm grew stronger, Bill saw the possibility that his son might have a career as a pitcher. He even built a field, complete with baseball diamond and bleachers, on their farm. Because Bob was shy, Bill eased him into competition so he could build up his confidence.

He did, and after a few years, Bob had become so aggressive that he was routinely striking out a dozen or more batters each game. Major league scouts took notice. In 1936, at age 17, Bob Feller amazed the baseball world by striking out 15 St. Louis Browns in his first start for the Cleveland Indians. In that rookie season, he struck out 76 batters in 62 innings. His fastball, estimated at 102 miles per hour, provoked his legend as one of the hardest throwing pitchers in history.

He was an extremely hard worker. Among his list of achievements: leading the league in innings pitched five times, in wins six times, and in strikeouts seven times. He could pitch a complete game one day, and get back in the bullpen only a day or two later.

Feller was also busy in the off season. He kept up a rigorous program of physical fitness all year, not waiting until spring training to get in shape. He organized barnstorming tours around the country with other top players, and people packed the ballparks to see them. He became one of the wealthiest players of his generation.

"Winners change. Losers make the same mistakes and complain."

5. Initiative

Because of his poor eyesight, inventor Charles Kettering had to drop out of college twice, but he considered his condition an asset rather than a liability. "It keeps me from reading all the theories that tell why things can't be done," he once said. After graduation, he joined the National Cash Register Company and started working on the first electric cash register.

Kettering approached inventing differently than others. Instead of hanging around with fellow inventors or with company executives, he talked with salesmen in the field and with the people who would use the product. Always practical, he kept a close eye on costs as well as on the marketplace. Later, with a former NCR vice-president, he founded Dayton Engineering Laboratories (DELCO) and began work on his most famous invention, the electric car ignition.

It was 1908, and drivers at the time were using hand cranks to start their cars, which would often stall in traffic. Kettering took his device to carmakers the following year; Cadillac expressed strong interest and ordered 8,000 units. At the time, Kettering and his associates were working out of a barn. They had no manufacturing facilities. The common wisdom among engineers was that Kettering's design broke every law of electrical engineering, to which he replied that he hadn't broken any laws, but simply made his device 90% automotive and 10% electrical.

Kettering eventually sold Delco to General Motors and continued to work for them for the next three decades. He made a large fortune with blue chip investments, and he lost a small fortune in risky new technologies, including new gasoline engines, aircraft design, and a steel tennis racket company.

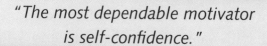

"The most dependable motivator is self-confidence."

Twelve years before Lewis and Clark crossed the continent, Scottish-born Alexander Mackenzie made his own journey from Montreal through the Canadian wilderness, finding his way to both the Pacific and Arctic oceans. He learned French so he could communicate with the men on the expedition, and he studied native tongues so he could communicate with the Indian guides. His purpose was simple: to make a lot of money in the fur trading business.

In his journal Mackenzie wrote: "I not only contemplated the practicability of penetrating across the continent of America, but was confident in the qualifications, as I was animated by the desire to undertake the perilous enterprise."

Mackenzie and his men traveled some 30 miles a day, canoeing down rushing rivers and carrying equipment over terrain so rugged that their moccasins would wear out in a day. When the expedition of 1789 failed to find a route to the Pacific, he sailed back to England for a year of training in navigation, astronomy and geography. He sought out other explorers to learn what he could from them. Then he set out again.

This time, he was successful. On reaching the Pacific shore, he mixed his own ink from vermilion and melted grease and on the face of a large rock wrote: "Alexander Mackenzie. From Canada. By Land. 22nd July 1793."

Later, he published his journals, which were best sellers, and was knighted by King George IV. It was Mackenzie's accomplishment that prompted the Lewis and Clark expedition.

"When somebody tells us 'no,' to me it just means 'I'll come back tomorrow.'"
—Noreen Jenkins, advocate for people with disabilities

For Major League slugger Ted Williams, hitting the ball was more a science than an art. As a rookie, he'd study everything pitchers did, wanting to know whether or not they were wild, and how long they'd last in a game. He aimed to understand them and anticipate their tendencies.

Whenever he approached the plate, Williams displayed amazing confidence, and he was always looking for a challenge, especially from pitchers who had gotten him out. On the last day of the 1941 season, he went into the game with a batting average of .39955, which was technically .400 but that was not good enough for him. When his manager offered to sit him down, Williams refused. He wanted to earn the .400, and he did, finishing the day six for eight.

> *"Never attack where the enemy expects you to come."*
> —George S. Patton, U.S. Army General

Pullman sleeping cars were the height of luxury in the era of train travel, and Pullman porters were the black men who worked in them. A small group of porters decided in 1925 to form a union,

even though the Pullman company was notoriously against them, and they called upon A.
Philip Randolph for help.

An outspoken, college-educated union organ-
izer and advocate of equal rights for blacks, Randolph took on the challenge. He scheduled a
series of speeches, the first of them at a New York
City meeting hall where, he knew, Pullman spies
were in the audience. Randolph stirred the audience with one simple idea: Together we have
power. The next day, 200 porters joined the union;
the Pullman company fired them.

Typically, the next move would have been to
take the porters out on strike, but Randolph understood that this was no ordinary case. Because
of prevalent racism, most of the porters saw their
jobs as being their only security, and Randolph
realized he would have to take his message to
them personally. He walked through the train stations, talking to the porters one by one. He visited
them at their homes and met their families. Eventually he was able to convince them that though
organizing was a risk, it would be worth it. It was
a long struggle, but in 1935, the American Federation of Labor voted to grant the union a charter,
and two years later the Pullman company signed
a contract, which Randolph negotiated and raised
support for every step of the way. In 1955, Randolph became a vice-president on the executive
council of the AFL-CIO.

6. Teamwork

Turn Conflict from Harmful to Healthful

Here's a word of advice from management coach Erik Van Slyke: Don't stifle conflict and don't impose solutions. Listen to what's behind the complaint and it may lead you to the underlying problem that needs to be solved.

Supervisors are particularly reluctant to deal with issues between employees and management. They don't see that conflict is actually an opportunity to improve relations with workers. Here are some suggestions:

~ Prepare to be a mediator by looking beyond what people are saying; get to what their interests or needs are.

~ Meet separately with employees in conflict before bringing them together. Establish a bond of trust and a position of neutrality.

~ In the group meeting or series of meetings, ask questions such as what they would like the meeting to accomplish, or what they would do if they were in the other person's shoes. Questions allow both parties to make their points.

~ Seek alternative solutions. Giving people control over their choices promotes teamwork, allowing them to piggyback ideas onto each other's suggestions.

~ Build a plan for implementing the solution. Schedule a future meeting to see how it is working.

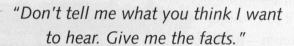

"Don't tell me what you think I want to hear. Give me the facts."

Army captains and explorers Meriwether Lewis and William Clark were a legendary team. When President Jefferson sent them to explore the new land acquisition known as the Louisiana Purchase, they hired a Frenchman to help guide their expedition. The guide brought along his wife, Sacagawea, a young Indian woman who had just given birth to a son.

Their journey from the Northern Great Plains to the Pacific Ocean took two years and four months, during which they faced blizzards, floods, hunger and illness, not to mention the constant danger of bears. Their survival depended upon how well they could live off the land. That's where the young Indian wife came in as the de facto third member of the leadership team.

Sacagawea served as interpreter, negotiator, and symbol of peace to the native tribes they encountered along the way. She also knew where to find roots and plants to supplement their diet. She has gone down in history for the role she played in the venture that preceded the opening of the West.

> *"If you prefer to do only what you are told, the order-givers will control your life."*

Florida State business professor Wayne Hockwarter surveyed 700 employees in a variety of jobs to find out why people quit—is it because of the job itself or because of the boss? The number one issue, he found, is bosses keeping their word. If trust is absent, a worker has no incentive to make the extra effort to do a job well. How do you foster that trust? Bosses should:

~ Have values which match the company's values.
~ Make expectations clear.
~ Make employees aware of change.
~ Be willing to admit mistakes.

7. Coping with Conflict and Adversity

As Secretary of State, Condoleezza Rice traveled to Egypt and spoke to an audience of students at American University in Cairo. In her speech, she made a number of stunning remarks as she pressed the case for democracy in the Muslim world. First, she addressed the audience as "ladies and gentlemen," offering them an equality which does not exist in that society. Then she answered the hostile critics of democracy.

To the charge that democracy leads to chaos, she maintained that the opposite is true: freedom overcomes hatred, division and violence. To the idea that economic and social progress can be achieved without free markets and minds, she said that human potential is fully realized only when governments trust their people's decisions and invest in their futures. Rice acknowledged that the United States had for 60 years been pursuing stability in the Middle East at the expense of democracy. That was going to change.

It was, said one journalist, "a golden moment in American foreign policy, unassailable by either the left or the right at home."

"The crisis of today is the joke of tomorrow."

He grew up a bullied "mama's boy" in the teeming slums of New York and died of a rare neurological disease before his 38th birthday. Between that difficult beginning and tragic end, Lou Gehrig became the "Iron Horse" of baseball, putting together a record 2,130 consecutive games over 14 seasons. Even after his illness forced him to retire from the game, he declared he was "the luckiest man on the face of the earth."

> *"Success is a lousy teacher.*
> *It seduces smart people into thinking*
> *they can't lose. "*
> —Bill Gates, Microsoft founder

Newspaper publisher Edward Scripps believed that setbacks in life are really opportunities that can serve to make a person stronger. The founder of the successful Cleveland Penny Press tried to launch a newspaper in St. Louis, but he ran up against competition from Joseph Pulitzer's Post-Dispatch. Such a well-established newspaper proved too formidable for Scripps' fledgling enterprise, and the paper folded. Later, when his newspaper chain faced a threat from rival Associated Press, Scripps said, "I have always counted it a piece of distinct good fortune when we encountered some disaster . . . that compels us to fall back again upon our old faith and upon our individual resources."

Scripps-Howard became the largest newspaper chain of the early 20th century; its syndication service, United Press Association, was the forerunner of United Press International.

Dan Mazur was 28,000 feet up Mt. Everest, just short of the peak, when he came upon another climber, Lincoln Hall, who had been left for dead by his party. Mazur found Hall sitting on the brow of a ridge in the minus 20 degree air with no gloves or hat and with his jacket unzipped. The lack of oxygen had disoriented him; he thought he was on a boat.

Mazur had his own party to take to the summit, but he couldn't abandon Hall. He bundled the man back into his clothing, gave him some Snickers bars and water, and oxygen from a spare tank. Then he radioed the base camp and waited four hours for help to arrive.

Mazur never made it to the top. The four hours they had lost made it risky to go on. Still, his rescue of Hall made him front page news, and Mazur said, "I'm humbled, very humbled, by the whole thing."

"Pain is usually the price for gain."

9

Luck Is a Ghost

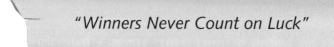

"Winners Never Count on Luck"

To depend on luck means that we think of life as a gamble. Nothing could be more misleading. Rather, I have come to believe that we find success and happiness only when we learn to recover from bad times. The key is to literally rescue ourselves when bad things happen.

The Benefits of Self Rescue

Winners have learned to recover—rescue themselves when they fall behind, get lost or find themselves losing. This self-rescue knowledge provides a great competitive advantage because it:

- Decreases dependence on others
- Increases confidence

- Encourages risk taking
- Prompts improvement
- Stimulates initiative
- Overcomes apathy
- Counters resistance to change
- Enhances self esteem
- Test values
- Attracts loyalty

Deciding to never count on luck prompts us to:

~ Find Ways to Bring Out Our Best
~ Overcome Apathy
~ Resist the Temptation to Retreat
~ Decrease Dependence
~ Rise Above Conditions
~ Avoid Bureaucratic Inertia
~ Associate with Tenacious People
~ Realize the Benefits of Cooperation
~ Appreciate the Value of Thoroughness and Quality
~ Create New / Untried Options

1. Find Ways to Bring Out Our Best

> "An education is not 'delivered'
> via teaching in classrooms or even
> with books and computers, but in
> building on every experience
> every day."

Life as a midshipman trainee in the 18th century Royal British Navy was nasty and brutal, featuring cramped quarters below the waterline, scant food, and the threat of disease everywhere. George Vancouver survived six years of that ordeal, passed his exam for a commission, and began a series of world-wide trips. During his career, he mapped all the harbors of the Caribbean, sailed to the Pacific Northwest and surveyed the entire Hawaiian Islands chain. He became one of the youngest warship captains, known not only for his rigorous self-discipline and dedication, but also for his wisdom.

These accomplishments are even more astounding in light of the fact that all his life Vancouver suffered from Grave's disease, a hyperthyroid condition characterized by fatigue, shakiness, anxiety, weight loss and sleep difficulties.

A six volume memoir of his *Voyage of Discovery to the North Pacific Ocean and Round the World* was published after his death in 1798.

> *"A winner is someone who recognizes his God-given talents, works his tail off to develop them into skills, and uses these skills to accomplish his goals"*
> —Larry Bird, basketball player

So Young, So Good

Johnny Bench's plaque in Baseball's Hall of Fame reads he "redefined standards by which catchers are measured." His records prove it. During his first year as catcher for the Cincinnati Reds in 1968, he was selected the National League Rookie of the Year and went on to win his first of 10 consecutive Gold Glove Awards. In 1970, he hit 48 home runs with 148 runs batted in, records which still stand today. He was 22 at the time.

In 1972, Johnny received bad news from his doctors. They had discovered a spot on his lung. Not to be deterred, he went on to play in the World Series and won the National League's

Most Valuable Player award. The best of all he learned he was cancer free. When Bench retired in 1983 at age 35, he had been voted an All-Star 14 times. In 1989, he was inducted into the Hall of Fame with nearly 97% of votes.

Proctor & Gamble CEO A. G. Lafley believes that every failure is an opportunity to learn. "We just want the learning to occur early, fast and cheap," he says, "not after billions of dollars are invested." Named one of America's best leaders by Harvard's Kennedy School of Government, Lafley prefers to be an agent for change, encouraging people to take the minority side of an issue rather than having them advocate for the most popular or immediate solution. Uncompromising integrity is his bottom line—in the moral sense, and in thought and action. "Sort through flattery, through politics," he advises, "come to grips with reality, and then bring incredible integrity to the decision and the action."

2. Overcome Apathy

> *"Discipline always prevails over wishes."*

When tragedy strikes, some people find it easier to just throw up their hands and surrender. Then there's Ruth Fertel. A few months after the divorced mom purchased Chris Steak House—which she did by mortgaging her home—a hurricane came through New Orleans and left her with no electricity and a cooler full of steaks. Rather than let them spoil, she cooked up a bunch of dinners and served them to disaster victims and workers in the community. Many became loyal customers, and Fertel's 60-seat business prospered. On a busy night people waited two hours for a table.

Then, ten years later, a fire destroyed the restaurant. In tears, she called her bank to relay the news and let them know she had found a new location. A construction contractor, in the bank at the time, overheard the conversation and said he could get the new place ready in a week.

The new restaurant had 160 seats, and—without the wait—customers started coming through the door in droves. Ruth's Chris Steak House, as it was now known, was thriving once again. By 1997, through opening additional locations and selling franchises, Fertel was presiding over a 59-unit operation with annual sales of $205 million.

"I find television very educational. Every time someone switches it on, I go to another room and read a good book."

—Groucho Marx, comedian

In the volatile world of popular music, Kenny Rogers' long career is something of an anomaly. The Texas native has chalked up 22 Number One hits, and earned a total of 45 prestigious awards, including 18 American Music Awards and three Grammies. How has he managed to stay on the charts through five decades? By not resting on his accomplishments. Acknowledging that he is not a particularly great singer, Rogers attributes his success to being able to find great songs. Critics add that he is a great communicator of songs, conveying to the listener every nuance of emotion. He still has the ability to surprise people and challenge himself.

Bobby Vinton is another music survivor. Beginning with a string of hit songs in the early years of rock—"Roses Are Red," "Mr. Lonely," "Blue Velvet"— the singer has retained his popularity through the decades by establishing himself as a top concert performer. A versatile entertainer, he is able to draw huge audiences in venues that range from Las Vegas and Atlantic City to cities around the country and even overseas. Vinton formed his first band as a teenager and worked his way through college, earning a degree in composition from Duquesne University, which also awarded him an honorary doctorate.

3. Resist the Temptation to Retreat

"Isn't it interesting that, looking back, we believe the obstacles we overcame give us an advantage now. "

With his fearless on-the-scene reporting and straight-from-the-shoulder delivery, broadcast journalist Edward R. Murrow was popular with audiences. But he made his bosses nervous. After describing the horrific condition of the prisoners at Buchenwald when the concentration camp was liberated, he told his listeners, "If I have offended you by this rather mild account, I'm not the least sorry." He criticized the Communist-hunting Sen. Joseph McCarthy on national television. He conducted an investigative report about a Texas land scandal involving one of his program's own sponsors, Alcoa.

Network executives repeatedly urged Morrow to "tone it down," but he believed that journalists have a duty to be accurate. He urged colleagues to guard against the temptation to become complacent, or indifferent. He once said this about the medium of television: "This instrument can teach

. . . but only to the extent that humans are determined to use it to those ends."

Sensational Substitute

A well-known fact in many team sports is the critical need for substitute players. This was clearly
illustrated in the Korean War, when the U.S.
forces chief ground commander was killed and
replaced by an Army deputy chief of staff at the
Pentagon. Although viewed as an Administrator,
Matthew Ridgway quickly showed his skills as a
Commander. Then, when President Truman removed General Douglas MacArthur, he appointed Ridgway as Commander of all U.N.
forces in Korea.

Unlike the Generals before him, Ridgway
wanted to find out why battles were lost. He
talked with soldiers in the field and studied the
terrain. He put black and white soldiers in the
same battalion. If soldiers' hands were cold, he
passed out gloves. If his Officers weren't on the
front lines, if they thought more about defensive
than offensive strategies, they were soon replaced. In other words, he got his hands dirty.
Morale improved and fighting in Korea ended in
1953.

Lt Col. George Collins writing in the Air University Review reported Ridgway's instructions,
"I repeated to the commanders as forcefully as I

could," he said "the ancient Army slogan. 'Find them! Fight them! Finish them!'"

Omar Bradley, former chairman of the Joint Chiefs of Staff in his book, *A General's Life,* paid him the ultimate compliment: "It is not often in wartime that a single battlefield commander can make a decisive difference. But in Korea, Ridgway would prove to be the exception. His brilliant, driving, uncompromising leadership would turn the tide of battle like no other general's in our military history."

> *"The only requirement for having and keeping abundance is to work long and hard in a <u>free</u> country."*

4. Decrease Dependence

Being blind does not discourage Erik Weihenmayer from climbing mountains—literally. He scaled Oregon's Mt. Hood in 2003 and Mt. Everest the following year. What's the attraction for someone who cannot see the view? For Weihenmayer, it's the challenge of figuring out how much he can do with the abilities he has. "Life isn't fair," he says, "You've just got to take what happens and make it work for you."

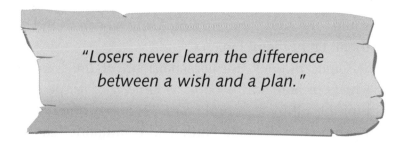

"Losers never learn the difference between a wish and a plan."

No Excuses

Eddie Robinson would accept no excuses when it came to his dream of becoming a football coach. He studied hard and in 1941 at only 22, became a football coach at the then all-black Grambling State University in Louisiana. Robinson instilled his winning determination in his players. His philosophy was clear and direct – "We will practice, practice, practice until we get it right." After 57 years in coaching, he had amassed over four hundred victories, a record in college football history.

Savvy—Getting and Keeping It

You can hire an expert for almost anything, or you can develop your own expertise. Here's how to educate yourself in your field:

- ~ Read your industry journals; join a professional association.
- ~ Use the Internet to research innovations in your market or profession.
- ~ Initiate dialogue. Ask customers and potential customers what issues concern them; let

them know when one of your new products
or services matches their need.

~ Attend seminars and conferences; take advantage of training offered.

~ Try new products and techniques; invest in tools that help you perform optimally.

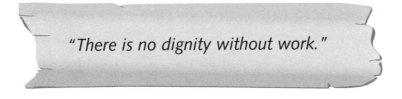

"There is no dignity without work."

5. Rise Above Conditions

Two fishing fanatics decided to try ice fishing. On their return, the wife of one of them asked, "How did it go?"

"It was a waste of time," he said wearily. "We kept cutting the hole bigger and bigger, but we never could get the boat through."

Colin Powell achieved both honor and fame as
Chairman of the Joint Chiefs of Staff and as Secretary of State. His roots, however, were humble.
Powell grew up in New York City, in the South
Bronx, graduated from its public schools, and
went on to the City College of New York. He
was not a gifted student, and after dropping out
of the engineering program, he went into geol-

ogy because it was the easiest way to get a degree.

Powell's relatives were immigrants from Jamaica who worked hard at low wage jobs so that their children could become doctors, lawyers and engineers. He remembers them saying, "You will not be allowed to disappoint us. You will do something with your life." They were mystified by his choice of the military as a career, though Powell liked the training and the structure. His parents stopped second guessing him when he became a general. They could also point with pride to his bronze star, purple heart, and distinguished service medals, which he earned for service in Viet Nam.

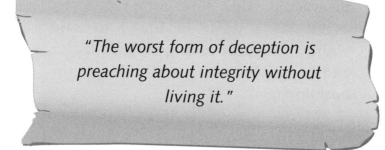

"The worst form of deception is preaching about integrity without living it."

What's wrong with conflict? Nothing!

In fact, with the right focus, a valuable outcome can emerge. "Differences can be the key to creative ideas and creative problem solving," says Tim Flanagan, co-author with Craig Runde of, *Becoming a Conflict Competent Leader.* To manage conflict effectively:

~ Deal with it expeditiously—differences become misunderstandings, which can lead to disagreements, discord and an entrenchment of positions.

~ Remain calm and stick to facts—think before you act.

~ Try to see things from the other person's point of view.

Dan Dana, author of *Managing Differences*, says that most conflicts have a "triggering event" that may cause a person to feel threatened and become angrily defensive. His advice:

~ Prevent conflict escalating to retaliation by catching it early.

~ Mediate with face-to-face communication.

~ Authorize employees to solve their own problems.

6. Avoid Bureaucratic Inertia

Reinventing a company that is 100 years old takes more than courage; it takes energy and vision. When Jeffrey Immelt was tapped to be CEO of General Electric in 2001, he might have ridden on the coattails of the previous and highly successful CEO, Jack Welch. But Immelt saw even further room for improvement. His agenda included repositioning GE's portfolio of businesses, spinning off lower return assets and buying entertainment and biotech firms to generate growth. He altered the corporate culture, too, making it more diverse, global and customer driven. Wall Street took notice, sending GE's stock price up nearly 20 percent.

> *"Mediocre minds seek and support selfish causes."*

As a young man, Chris Kraft went to work for the National Advisory Committee for Aeronautics, and found himself butting heads with future astronaut John Glenn, who was then a Defense Department liaison. At issue was a problem with the wings of a new fighter jet. Kraft's data told him where the problem was, but Glenn had doubts and ordered additional tests at different altitudes. After several more tests, whose results Glenn also disbelieved, Kraft had had enough. Refusing to subject test pilots to further dangers, he went over Glenn's head and straight to an admiral, who ordered the aircraft grounded immediately.

Kraft's instincts about making decisions served him well years later, when he became NASA's flight director for all of the Mercury and Gemini flights into outer space.

> *"Winning without merit is an accident unlikely to be repeated."*

7. Associate with Tenacious People

> *"Growth depends not on a single victory but on continuing effort."*

After hiding for three years in the jungles of Viet Nam to escape capture by the communist North Vietnamese army, Lapthe Flora escaped on a rickety, overcrowded boat. The teenager spent a year in a refugee camp in Indonesia before being adopted by an American couple and brought to this country. His challenges continued as he struggled to learn English and adapt to his new life, but with daily study and practice, he became fluent in the language, then set his sights on furthering his education. He earned a bachelor's degree in pre-med studies from the Virginia Military Institute and, as part of his obligation to the college, served in the National Guard.

Though Flora's hopes of becoming a doctor ended when he could not achieve the necessary high grades, he used his knowledge of chemistry and physics to land a job in the Night Vision unit of ITT Industries. The company agreed to train him to become an engineer, and Flora found himself rising through the ranks of ITT as well as the National Guard simultaneously. He received the National Guard's Gen. Douglas MacArthur Award for Leadership in 1995. A few years later, he was tapped by his employer to head a new department for business development.

Flora has taken away some lesson from every part of his life. In Vietnam, he learned the ethic of hard work. Struggling for survival in the jungle, he often wanted to scream out loud but remembered there were people in worse situations. Finding success in this country, he says, "You have opportunities everywhere. Things might be difficult, but not impossible."

"Never, ever underestimate the potential of those who have proved they can overcome severe hardship or handicap."

James Lewis Kraft had just $65 in capital and a rented horse-drawn wagon when, fresh from a failed partnership, he went into the cheese business for himself. In the early days of the 20th century, grocery stores had 60 pound hunks of cheddar sitting under a glass bell on their counters. Every morning they would have to carve away and discard the dried out surfaces, which made it difficult for them to earn a profit. Kraft wasn't profiting either. Before long, he found himself $3,000 in debt.

But Kraft had an attitude that would not let him quit. He decided that he would help the merchants avoid the waste by selling them only as much cheese as they could sell. He went to the wholesale market early each day to get the best cheese and delivered it personally. Soon he became known for the quality of his products, and he began packaging cheese under his name.

Kraft went further. Wanting to improve the shelf life of cheese, he set up a laboratory to study the issue, experimenting with a variety of cheeses, blending them and cooking them at different temperatures. By 1915, he was producing processed cheese in four-ounce tins, and they became an immediate success. The following year, he received a patent on the new product, and when the U.S. entered World War I, Kraft sold 6 million pounds of canned cheese to the armed forces.

At one point, when grocers became overstocked with 4- ounce and 8-ounce tins of cheese, instead of cutting production, Kraft offered them a matching rebate if they would cut their prices. The plan worked.

Today, Kraft Foods is one of the largest food companies in the world.

8. Realize the Benefits of Cooperation

How to Make Complicated Ideas Understandable

You're the expert, and people want to hear what you have to say, but explaining complicated ideas in terms that everyone can understand can be a challenge. Here are some tips from public relations consultant David Silver, an advisor in the areas of finance and investor relations:

- ~ Relate your topic to everyday human experience. Can you describe an economic event in terms of the price rise of a common grocery item, for example?
- ~ Use a visual tool—such as a graph, flow chart or pyramid—to demonstrate different levels or steps in a process.
- ~ Break the information up into manageable units and offer them point by point, allowing listeners time to absorb each one. You can also propose a series of questions, which you answer in sequence.

~ Begin at the end. Summarize your most important idea so that people understand what you want them to take away from your talk.

"Always take a second look at what seems to be accurate."

Friendly Persuasion

Winning others to your point of view is a basic imperative of business. In, *Persuasion: The Art of Getting What You Want,* author Dave Lakhani advises starting with a provocative statement or question to grab your audience's attention. From there, it's a balancing act between giving too little information, which will confuse people, and too much, which will bore them. Here are a few of his suggestions:

~ Target the action steps you want your listeners to take.

~ Use humor; it's a natural breaker of barriers.

~ Set deadlines for milestones; if you fail to convince someone within a specified time, move on.

Jack Griffin, communications coach and author

of *How to Say It at Work,* offers these additional ideas for gaining consensus:

~ Find allies and keep their support.
~ Focus on broad areas of agreement, even though methods may differ.
~ Encourage candid feedback and weave it into your proposal.

And Samuel Bachrach, author of *Get Them on Your Side,* weighs in with these tips:

~ Sell the benefits: tell others what they will get from your plan.
~ If you can't convert the opposition, keep them from undermining your efforts.

> *"Complex plans attract less understanding, fewer advocates and poor results."*

9. Appreciate the Value of Thoroughness and Quality

Give Them What They Want

Two of my wife and daughters' favorite magazines are "Taste of Home" and "Simple and Delicious." They are upbeat, concise cooking magazines filled with delicious recipes. Published by Reiman Publications both rose to be in the nation's top 100 magazines. Roy Reiman and his wife Bobbi began their publishing business in the basement of their home. After several missteps, they saw a need for publications about rural life, farming, small towns, cooking and nature. They aimed their magazines towards those markets and business soared. The evidence? In 2002, Reader's Digest bought Reiman Publications for $760 million.

"When hope is unquenchable and persistence prevails, success will surely follow."

John Wooden is considered the greatest college basketball coach—and possibly the greatest coach in any sport—having led the UCLA men's basketball team to a record 10 NCAA championships. He was one of only three men to be inducted into the Basketball Hall of Fame as both a player and a coach.

Though Wooden was strict and demanding, his most powerful attribute was his credibility. He led by example, and whatever he asked of his players was not more than what he demanded of himself. He never raised his voice or used profanity, and he never imposed his will. He asked the men on his team to be moral citizens, to display compassion and decency for all people, to work hard on and off the basketball court.

"I believe effective leaders are, first and foremost, good teachers," he said. His secret to success: "Little things done well." To lay that foundation, he ran his players through regular practices and drills. He wanted them to believe the best way to improve the team was to improve themselves and perform to the best of their ability. After every game and practice, he would sit down with them and offer encouragement and advice. He wanted them to take pride in a job well done.

At age 95 and long retired from coaching basketball, Wooden was still delivering his message, giving some 30 motivational speeches a year to various organizations. In 2003 he received the Presidential Medal of Freedom.

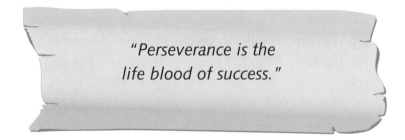

"Perseverance is the life blood of success."

10. Create New/Untried Options

Eternal Optimist

The old saying "you can't keep a good man down" applies perfectly to William Piper. Knowing little about airplanes, Piper took a $400 investment during the trying economic times of the 1930's, and built the low cost Piper Cub. To encourage sales, he offered his employees and customers free flying lessons. He constantly enhanced the plane to make it more attractive to potential buyers. He saw a big market in the U.S. military, but the attack on Pearl Harbor in 1941 made his point. Because Cubs were small, lightweight and easy to maneuver they quickly became effective warplanes in specific situations. He even encouraged civilians to use their Cubs as an auxiliary to the Air Force. At the time of his death in 1970, Piper had produced more planes than any other aircraft manufacturer. In 1981, he was elected to the Aviation Hall of Fame.

"I learned more from the one restaurant that didn't work than from all the ones that were successes."
—Wolfgang Puck, chef, restauranteur

If a company does not innovate, it risks being considered behind the times; but any innovation runs the risk of tinkering with success. Mike Lazaridis is the man behind Research In Motion, which is the company that launched the Black-Berry wireless device. Since founding RIM in 1984, Lazaridis has had to constantly weigh one set of risks against another.

BlackBerry had already earned a solid reputation as a communications tool for high-powered professionals when Lazaridis decided to launch the Pearl, a smart phone newly designed with a built-in camera and digital music player. Analysts worried that the new device would not only dilute the brand image, it would burden the company with costly R&D and force it into price competition with other consumer electronics products.

Entrepreneurial and hands-on though he is, Lazaridis does not hesitate to solicit ideas from his designers and engineers in weekly "vision meetings." He also shares leadership responsibilities with a co-CEO, whose experience in finance balances Lazaridis' engineering background. With all that input, Lazaridis felt confident that the new BlackBerry Pearl would be a success. With its thinner body and bright screen, the Pearl can compete with more sleekly designed models such as Motorola's. And it is positioned in the same way as all of RIM's products are: to awe users and improve their lives.

"The way to get good ideas is to get lots of ideas and throw the bad ones away."

—Linus Pauling, chemist

10

Up and At 'Em

Ultimately, we are able to stand and deliver over time because we have learned:

How to Become Unstoppable.

Here are the rules:

1. Never allow fear to prevent you from trying.
2. Realize that only you control what you can become.
3. Tolerate pain and you will hurt less.
4. Try new ways.
5. Accept that:

   ~ Your accomplishments are what you have overcome or improved.
   ~ Gifts are the opposite of achievements.
   ~ All admiration is fleeting. It's a what-have-you-done-for-me-lately world.

6. Believe tomorrow will be better.

This conduct is not easy because it demands:

~ *Self-control and direction* to keep going.

~ *Integrity* to resist misconduct, which is tempting.

~ *A positive attitude* to overcome rejection.

~ *Focus and concentration* on priorities.

~ *Relentless testing* of best effort.

Self Control and Direction

"Action is your mind in motion."

Most people know Earvin "Magic" Johnson for his prowess on the basketball court. Not many realize that he has used his sense of gamesmanship to help numerous small business people open Starbucks, TGI Friday's, and five movie theaters in the inner city. He was also behind a partnership with Washington Mutual that gave loans to minority families so they could buy new homes.

"Good habits in America make any man rich. Wealth is a result of habit."
—John Jacob Astor, real estate developer

In the late 1980s, before the Internet made this a much smaller world and people became comfortable ordering gourmet food by mail, Dan Zawacki dreamed up a business idea that made him a laughingstock of bankers. The young man wanted to sell live lobster dinners, delivered directly to a customer's door, from Chicago. Unable to find any investors to back the venture, he maxed out eight gold credit cards and used another two to finance the interest charges. He got his company up and running, despite the general consensus that he was crazy, that his plan was never going to work.

Zawacki's lobster idea was hatched when he was a salesman for Honeywell in Peoria, Illinois. One year he decided to purchase live lobsters as holiday gifts and ship them to his customers. They were such a big hit, he wondered if there might be a need for a company that would handle all the buying and shipping. And so, Lobster Gram was born. Zawacki made up a hand-drawn ad and placed it in two major business magazines. They failed, so he maneuvered radio airtime on a popular station by offering to give away a few lobsters. That generated 180 orders. Soon, he found himself working 10 hour days, seven days a week. He was fired from Honeywell when his boss heard him on the radio plugging lobsters when he was supposed to be making sales calls.

Through additional radio ads and personal referrals, word slowly spread. People still had to be educated about ordering live lobsters by mail. On a good day, he would send out three orders. In 1996, he launched a web site and opened a warehouse near Boston, from where he shipped the live lobsters. Later, he began sending an annual 40-page color catalog to a mailing list of 550,000.

These days, Lobster Gram has expanded its offering to include lobster tails, filet mignon, seafood soups and gourmet desserts. Regardless of the economic climate, sales have been good, growing at a rate of 20-30 percent a year.

"If you know your enemies and know yourself, you will not be imperiled in a hundred battles; if you do not know your enemies but do know yourself, you will win one and lose one; if you do not know your enemies nor yourself, you will be imperiled in every single battle."

—Sun Tzu, Chinese philosopher

Integrity

In the mid-1980s, Tom Daniels was running a thriving general contracting company when an opportunity caught his eye. A neighbor had a business selling machines that turned ice into a powder to blend with the syrups that make snow cones. Daniels offered to sell the machines, and within a few months he placed them in Utah's largest department stores. Then, he approached *Back to Basics, a* house wares manufacturing company, where he soon became a partner heading their sales department.

Over the next decade, Daniels regularly launched new product lines at various price points and became the company's president and CEO. In 2000, he invented a smoothie maker, dubbed the Smoothie Elite, which soon took away a huge part of the market for blenders. His company also developed with a popcorn maker and other cooking products, all centered around the theme "family, food and fun."

In 2005, Daniels stepped down as CEO, feeling that it was time to let other capable team members "run with the ball." At the time, the company's annual revenues had reached $67 million.

"The activist is not the man who says the river is dirty. The activist is the man who cleans up the river."

—Ross Perot, entrepreneur

At 5′ 11″ and 200 pounds, Pat Tillman wasn't large enough to play football—or so everyone thought. After earning a spot as a starter for Arizona State University, no one expected him to: 1) be named Pac-10 defensive player of the year and lead his team to the 1997 Rose Bowl, or 2) turn down a multimillion dollar contract with the NFL Arizona Cardinals to enlist in the military . . . but he did!

Material possessions did not matter to Tillman. Achievement did. He was proud of earning a university degree because, as a mediocre student, he had to work so much harder to get good grades. In 2001 he turned down a $9 million, five-year offer from the St. Louis Rams and accepted instead a $500,000 one-year contract from the Cardinals because he felt grateful to the Cardinals for their faith in signing him right out of college.

Tillman was killed in Afghanistan in 2004. His father's tribute: "Pat was always testing himself."

> *"Lincoln was not great because he was born in a log cabin, but because he got out of it."*
>
> —James Truslow Adams, historian

When he died in 323 B.C. at the age of 32, Alexander the Great ruled over a great swath of the known world. His empire stretched from Greece to Central Europe and the Balkans, and from Northern Africa through most of Asia and part of India. Though Alexander came from a line of warriors and these were conquered lands, he was so benevolent a ruler that none of his occupied territories ever rebelled. He attempted to understand the people he ruled, observed local customs wherever he traveled, and was so impressed with the Egyptian judicial system that he ordered all laws in his kingdom to be compatible with it.

Where did Alexander get the wisdom to rule in a way none before—and few after—have done? He was tutored by the philosopher Aristotle, who used the method of his teacher, Socrates. It taught him the importance of approaching a problem by asking the right questions, and to rely on information from a number of sources. In battles, he required intelligence not only from his officers, but also from experts we now call meteorologists, engineers, botanists and zoologists. Only then did he decide the best time to invade, how many troops could be supported in an area, and how conquering one region might help him the next time. In determining the best route to take over a mountain, for example, the advice of a shepherd might be better than that of an officer. Alexander led from the front lines, as all good leaders do. He entrusted his officers to act on their own once a strategy was agreed upon. Still good advice today.

In the midst of all the corporate greed we hear about daily, it's refreshing to read the following excerpt from a November 2, 2006 letter that Whole Foods CEO John Mackey sent to "all team members:"

". . . The tremendous success of Whole Foods Market has provided me with far more money than I ever dreamed I'd have and far more than is necessary for either my financial security or personal happiness. . . . I have reached a place in my life where I no longer want to work for money, but simply for the joy of the work itself and better answer the call to service that I feel so clearly in my own heart."

Mackey reduced his salary to $1 a year, donated all future stock options he would be eligible to receive to two company foundations, and set up a Global Team Member Emergency Fund to which the company would contribute $100,000 annually.

Positive Attitude

Pierre Omidyar's great faith in the goodness of people allowed him to launch eBay in 1995, at a time when the vast majority of Americans felt uncomfortable using a credit card online. Omidyar's challenge was to instill trust in a virtual marketplace and, because of the site's auction format, he also had to get total strangers to trust each other.

From the beginning, eBay relied on people's good nature. "Some people are dishonest. Or deceptive," Omidyar said. "But those people can't hide [on eBay]. We'll drive them away. Protect each other from them." The Feedback Forum, the site's message board, is the tool that allows registered users to rate a buyer or seller and write comments about transactions, thereby alerting other users to potential trouble.

After the phenomenal success of eBay, which today has over 212 million registered users worldwide and handles over $40 billion worth of goods every year, Omidyar launched Omidyar Network to fund micro loans for entrepreneurs in developing countries.

*"Before you curse your troubles,
walk through a cemetery."*

In the face of fierce competition from home improvement store behemoths Home Depot and Lowe's, Ray Griffith just smiles. The ACE Hardware CEO says, "All our vital signs are very positive, and people seem to be almost amazed at that." The numbers back him up. ACE has outperformed its two rivals in same store sales growth for four of the last five years.

Founded in 1924 by four Chicago-area hardware store owners who came together for mutual economic benefit, ACE is now a cooperative of 4,600 independent retailers that operate under the ACE banner in every state in the U.S. as well as 70 countries around the world. They manage to thrive because they fill a niche in the marketplace, catering to shoppers who appreciate personal service and brighter, easier-to-navigate stores.

"We come to work every day on behalf of the entrepreneur," says Griffith. "We have a chip on our shoulder about the big boxes, and we like that. We like being the underdog. America loves the underdog."

"As soon as you believe you can't compete—you can't."

Reuben Mattus was a small, independent New York City ice cream manufacturer, and he was getting tired of having his products crowded out of the grocery stores by the big manufacturers. Fifty years ago, ice cream was made from nonfat dry milk, artificial flavors and stabilizers, and bulked up with air. Mattus kept coming up with new products and packages, which ended up being copied by his rivals.

Mattus was no stranger to adversity. At the age of 11, he used a pushcart to take the iced lemon treats his widowed mother made to stores in his neighborhood. He dropped out of high school before graduation to work full time in the family business.

After years of trying to keep pace with the competition, Mattus decided to create a premium brand using real cream, fresh egg yolks and natural flavors. It would be heavier than conventional brands and cost three times as much. He launched the new line in 1961 and called it Haagen-Dazs, a name that meant nothing but gave the product a Danish, gourmet-sounding cachet.

Conventional supermarkets refused to carry the high-priced product, so Mattus and his wife, Rose, targeted stores in college towns, where the brand quickly developed a cult following by the rebellious youth of that era. This was not their father's ice cream. Meanwhile, Mattus kept on perfecting his product—he spent six years experimenting to find the right strawberry flavor—and Haagen-Dazs enthusiasts kept spreading the word. Soon, mainstream customers began adopting the ice cream as an affordable luxury.

By the early 1980s, Haagen-Dazs had become famous for its uncompromising quality. Sales were growing at double digits while the rest of the industry remained flat. In 1983, the company was bought by Pillsbury for over $70 million.

> *"Courage is not winning—
> it is trying against the odds."*

Focus on Priorities

Both Jeffrey Immelt, current CEO of General Electric Co., and Jack Welch, his predecessor, have a voracious appetite for reading. They know that good leaders are curious people, and they devote many hours to learning, thinking, and coming up with "imagination breakthroughs," as Immelt calls them. Good leaders are also obsessive about their workers. "When employees under perform, a leader tells them so," says Welch.

One of President Ronald Reagan's greatest strengths was that he kept his focus on what was important. After a particularly tense meeting in Geneva in 1985 with Soviet president Mikhail Gorbachev, Reagan angrily left the room. Then he stopped in the doorway, turned and calmly resumed his place at the table. "This isn't working," he told Gorbachev. "I would like to talk man to man, leader to leader, and see if we could really accomplish something worthwhile."

The resolution of conflict is much easier if the opposing parties find common ground, according to George Kohlrieser, author of *Hostage at the Table*, who offers these suggestions about how to do that:

~ Focus on your dreams and goals. Don't be afraid to raise issues; they can begin the dialogue toward resolution.

~ Ask yourself what has been lost in this situation—actual or anticipated.

~ Project yourself into the future. Do you see limits or possibilities? "Negative states shrink the mind's eye, while joy and satisfaction grow it," says Kohlrieser.

*"Hard work spotlights the character
of people: some turn up their sleeves,
some turn up their noses, and
some don't turn up at all."*
—Sam Ewing, writer

As a youngster, Terry Fox worked long summer days picking berries for his parents. His strong work ethic developed early and saw him through some very difficult days. During his freshman year in college he was diagnosed with bone cancer; doctors were going to remove his right leg. The night before his surgery, he read about an amputee who had completed the New York marathon. Fox, a varsity basketball player, vowed that not only would he do the same, he would raise money to help others with the disease. His plan was to run 26 miles a day across Canada, gathering donations for the Canadian Cancer Society a dollar at a time from each of that country's 24 million citizens.

After the surgery and six months of rehabilitation, Fox spent the next year and a half learning how to run on an artificial leg. When he began the marathon on April 12, 1980 in Newfoundland, the media had not yet picked up his story, and donations were slow in coming. At his last stop, though, he raised $10,000, a dollar from every resident of the town.

His daily schedule began at 5 A.M. with a four hour run, followed by a three hour break. He ran 12 to 16 miles each day, attracting more and more support along the way. When he reached the western end of the Great Lakes, he found that his cancer had returned, and he had to end the journey on September 1 to return home for more treatment. By that time, he had raised $1.7 million.

But now, 55 countries hold annual Terry Fox runs for cancer research, and his foundation has raised over $400 million. Fox died on June 28, 1981.

> *"Time is the scarcest resource, and unless it is managed, nothing else can be managed."*
>
> —Peter Drucker, management consultant and writer

Signs of the Times for Success in Business

Outdated Outlook	Priorities Needed Now
Memorized facts	Immediate data access
Locked-in goals	Agility
Social ties	Measurable accomplishments
Persuasive personality	Accountability
Lectures	Demonstrations and applications
Time consumed	Results achieved
Impression	Reality
Information gathered	Proven benefits
Training events	Development process
Degrees and credentials	Actual performance
Good intention	Difference made
Job stability	Flexibility
Seniority rules	Merit
Generalities	Focused expertise
Predictable promotion	Opportunistic risks
Quick fix	Persistence
Dependence	Self-discipline
Cookie cutter problem solving	Brainstorming
Tell me	Show me
Personal popularity	Authentic integrity

Relentless Best Effort

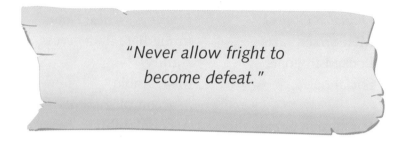

*"Never allow fright to
become defeat."*

Jordan Rubin was diagnosed with Crohn's disease, an incurable disorder of the intestines, when he was a 19-year-old college student. His weight dropped from 180 pounds to 105 pounds in a short time, and painful infections spread throughout his body. He sought help from some 70 health practitioners in 7 countries, without success. A specialist in New York City recommended removing his large intestine and part of the small intestine, advice he and his family rejected.

Then a nutritionist Rubin consulted believed that all he needed was a dramatic change in diet. Rubin ate nothing but fresh fruits and vegetables, freshly caught fish, and grass-fed beef for 40 days. When his symptoms began to subside, he knew he had found the answer to his illness. He kept to the diet, and by his 21st birthday his weight was back to normal and all his terrible symptoms were vanishing. A journalist wrote about his experience, and suddenly Rubin began receiving letters requesting information from thousands of doctors and patients.

Rubin went on to earn advanced degrees in nutrition and sports medicine, and later founded Garden of Life, a company that offers dietary supplements derived from nutrient-rich fresh foods. The year after the company was formed it had $2 million in revenues. Four years later, revenues were $58.5 million.

> *"To me, success can only be achieved through repeated failure and introspection. In total, success represents 1% of your work and results from the 99% that is called failure."*
> —Soichiro Honda, founder, Honda Corp.

Teddy Psychogios made his career in the hotel business. A Greek immigrant who spoke not a word of English, he got by at his first job as an elevator operator at the 23-story Sherman House in Chicago by reading the numbers on the guests' keys to get them to their floors. Later, at the LaSalle Hotel, he was a bellman and at age 21, became the youngest bell captain in the hotel's history. In those days, bellmen hustled for 50 cent tips to supplement their $5 a day salary. "We smiled a lot and worked hard," he said.

When he came to Chicago's Ritz–Carlton Hotel in 1978, Psychogios already had decades of experience under his belt, but the new clientele was more sophisticated, and expected only the best service. Psychogios became used to going that extra mile. For the next 27 years, he would cater to industrialists, bankers and celebrities as well as ordinary families on vacation. He knew scores of guests by name and learned their likes and dislikes. Example: he got the son of an executive an autograph from a basketball star because he knew how much the boy liked the sport. Some guests didn't call the front desk; they just contacted Psychogios and he handled things from there.

He has always followed the cardinal rule for Ritz-Carlton bellmen: "Don't wait to be asked."

Jack Hennessy was a rambunctious child and an excellent athlete who lived by the slogan: "Life is short. Play hard." Whatever he did, he gave all his effort, including service as a sergeant in the U.S. Army, fighting in Iraq. At his funeral in October 2004, a family member read an email sent by his company commander, which said in part: "Sergeant Jack Hennessy's team was always prepared and he was the most aggressive soldier on the battlefield."

I rest my case.

"All progress begins with two words—
Try Again."

Index

Additional Information

For more information about Dr. Roger Fritz's consulting and presentation topics or for a catalog of books, audio tapes, CD-ROMs, reprints, software and other products, contact:

Organization Development Consultants
Phone: 630.420.7673
Fax: 630.420.7835
Email: RFritz3800@aol.com
Website: http://www.rogerfritz.com